Bushwhacking

Bushwhacking

How to Get Lost in the Woods and Write Your Way Out

Jennifer McGaha

Trinity University Press
San Antonio, Texas

Trinity University Press
San Antonio, Texas 78212

Cover design by Derek Thornton / Notch Design
Book design by Amnet
Author photo by Avery McGaha

ISBN 978-1-59534-981-1 paper
ISBN 978-1-59534-982-8 ebook

Trinity University Press strives to produce its books using methods and materials in an environmentally sensitive manner. We favor working with manufacturers that practice sustainable management of all-natural resources, produce paper using recycled stock, and manage forests with the best possible practices for people, biodiversity, and sustainability. The press is a member of the Green Press Initiative, a nonprofit program dedicated to supporting publishers in their efforts to reduce their impacts on endangered forests, climate change, and forest-dependent communities.

The paper used in this publication meets the minimum requirements of the American National Standard for Information Sciences—Permanence of Paper for Printed Library Materials, ansi 39.48–1992.

CIP data on file at the Library of Congress
27 26 25 24 23 | 5 4 3 2 1

For my parents, James and Sue Heglar,
whose love for the outdoors sparked
a wildness in me early on.

And for all my students, past and present.
Walking the writing journey with
you has been one of the greatest honors of my life.

And into the forest I go, to lose my mind and find my soul.

—John Muir

CONTENTS

PREFACE

My grandfather was born and raised on a farm in the Sandy Mush community in Buncombe County, North Carolina, so deep in the country that at the local church cemetery, among the fading tombstones, a sign read "Burial by Permission Only." When he turned eighteen, he and my grandmother moved to downtown Canton in nearby Haywood County, and though he took a paying job as a crane operator at Champion International, he continued farming on their small plot of land. Thus, the country ways of being—the cycles of farming, of planting and harvesting and laying the field to rest—remained with him throughout his life. The autumn he was dying, he believed he was trapped in a snowstorm. He described the deep banks of snow, the bitter wind and icy roads. He had wrecked, he said, and needed a snowplow. Then, one October afternoon, in a rare moment of lucidity, he asked me, "Are the acorns falling yet?" It was a simple question, but filled with all the great ones: What season of life are we in? How do we find our way from one season to the next? And what do we do with the moments in between?

In the years since his death, I have come to believe that these questions are the crux of all good living and all good writing (as if the two can be separated!). What do we do on the page but seek to better understand where we have been and where we are headed, to learn how to move gracefully from one moment to the next? At times, this process feels a bit like leaving a clearly marked trail and embarking on your own into the wilderness. The term *bushwhacking* implies a physical thrashing about—slapping at branches, slicing through thickets, leaping over downed trees—but it also connotes a certain fortitude and resilience. It means leaving a relatively comfortable place and going where no path exists. It means embracing the unknowns of the forest. This, indeed, is the perfect metaphor for what memoir writers do every time we sit down to write. We slap at branches. We slice through thickets. We leap over downed trees. We walk in the footsteps of the writers who came before us, and we forge our own paths. My journeys through the woods, both literally and in my writing life, have filled me with mystery and amazement. They have also taught me to move through the world with a heightened state of awareness, which is to say, like a writer.

When I was a kid, my grandparents often took my brother and me to Gatlinburg, Tennessee. There, we would drive bumper cars and eat fudge and ride the chairlift, but the greatest thrill for me happened not in Gatlinburg but on the parkway along the way. I don't remember if we went at a certain time of day or if we always stopped at the same spot or if we went to different ones. I just remember an overlook with a rock wall, maybe three or four feet high. Just below that, wild black bears—often several at a time, sometimes mothers with cubs—waited to be fed. At the time, I did not know that feeding wild bears was a bad idea, and I doubt my grandparents did either. We were not overly enlightened in the seventies, and we simply saw some cute bears and thought, hey, why not? Aren't they really like giant, furry ducks?

When I think of this now, I wish I could say I am horrified. It was dangerous for us and for the bears, whose encounters with us may have emboldened them and made them aggressive with other humans. And yet the sweetness, the purity of this memory persists. I remember the thrill of riding in the back of the brown Nova, the windows rolled down, hot air whipping my hair, my grandfather's suntanned arm flung out the car window, my grandmother's plastic rain scarf cinched at her throat. I remember clutching between my sweaty thighs a Sunbeam bag full of heels of bread and stale saltine crackers. I remember how I could barely contain myself, how my brother could always contain himself. I remember his quiet grin, his barely-noticeable-if-you-did-not-know-him excitement, the way he sat on the edge of the vinyl seat, no seat belt, looking attentively out the front window in case my grandfather needed help with directions. My grandfather flicked on the turn signal and pulled to a stop near the rock wall. Outside the car, he lit a Camel and stood off to the side smoking and watching my grandmother, her creamy arms folded in front of her, her head thrown back as she laughed. Once, a bear reached up and took a cracker right from my hand.

"Careful, Junebug!" my grandfather called to me.

Almost five decades later, I can still smell the bear's musty scent, feel her rough tongue against my fingers, hear her guttural rumbling. I jumped back, startled, yes, but also delighted, entranced, consumed with a joy so pure my brain stored it safely away, marked it so that in the years to come, I could easily find it when I needed to conjure something marvelous.

This is, in part, I suppose, how this book came to be: an attempt to capture on the page something of the magic I have encountered in my life at a time when I have needed to be reminded that such magic exists. It has also been my attempt, following my grandfather's example, to ask the right questions, the big ones, the ones that really matter. After the election of 2016, like many Americans, I became increasingly dismayed and distraught by the state of our country, by the callousness and cruelty we witnessed night after night on the news (if we were lucky) or, worse, in our daily lives. And then, when the pandemic hit in 2020, I, along with the rest of the world, was forced to turn inward, to seek strength and solace in the places I always had—on the trail and on the page. Thus, somewhere along the way, this book that had begun in bits and pieces, in fits and starts over many years, finally began to coalesce.

This is not a book *about* the election, mind you. Nor is it a book about the pandemic. However, it is a book of the *season* of the pandemic, about the questions it raised for me, the ways I found my way through, and some of the truths I discovered along the way. Though some of the events described here happened long before Covid, I processed them during that time and through that lens. The long periods of stillness and solitude allowed me to reflect more deeply on the connections between my outdoor adventures and my writing life, and these essays probe what I learned during that time about the value of aloneness, of silence, of tenacity, of seeking joy and building community and embracing possibilities both seen and unseen. It was a time when my close-up vision was especially clear, my distance vision not so much. I focused, then, on what was in front of me, the things I knew most intimately: the woods, my family, my dogs, my imagination, and my memories. Every time I went into the woods, I learned something new, something that captivated and inspired me and somehow translated to my writing life.

Ask anyone who knows me well. I am generally a glass-half-empty sort of person, and positivity does not come easily for me. Therefore, it might surprise these people that I have written a book which, despite my natural inclinations, feels a bit like a rallying call for more optimism and joy in our writing lives. I know it has surprised me. Until recently, I believed upbeat people were just born that way—cooing, gurgling babies who grew up to be motivational speakers and church youth group leaders and heads of marketing teams and athletic organizations—like Ted Lasso but without the divorce-related angst. The process of writing this book, however, has taught me that being joyful is not a state of being. Rather, it is a practice, a way of moving through this world, and none of us will ever discover all that is possible if we cling stubbornly to our fears and doubts, if we stick only to the safe paths, the familiar, well-marked ones with no wild boars or stinging nettle or treacherous river crossings or deep ravines.

I am not overly brave in the conventional sense, but I have taken baby steps into claiming my own power, and you can too. There is nothing new in what I share here, no ground-breaking, insider tips about the writing life, nothing I'm saying that hasn't been said before in some other way. Perhaps there are no such revelatory ideas. Still, just as there are many ways of conjuring, there are many ways of getting at your particular truth, and my hope is that whether you love the outdoors or you freak at the sight of ticks or the sound of coyotes or the smell of stink bugs or the very notion of getting sweaty, you will find something of yourself in these pages, some expression of the ways you, too, have learned to be a little braver, a little stronger, a little more feral than you ever believed you could be.

The wildness in me honors the wildness in you.

May your writing, like your life, be a marvel.

WHY WE WRITE

Searching for Beauty

Caesars Head is a granite outcropping just over the North Carolina–South Carolina border. Created by shifting tectonic plates and water erosion, the rock is 3,266 feet above sea level and rests on the southern edge of the Blue Ridge Escarpment, the line where the Blue Ridge Mountains gives way to the South Carolina foothills. On a clear day, you can see three states from the top: North Carolina, South Carolina, and Georgia. You can buy a map and trinkets at the visitors' center. You can hike one of the trails in Jones Gap State Park in the Mountain Bridge Wilderness Area, a 13,000-acre forest. What you may not do, at least legally, is enter the park at night. There are too many obstacles to trip over, too many wild animals prowling about, too many ways to, like the dog the outcropping is allegedly named for, go tumbling off the mountain.

Nevertheless, on a bitterly cold night in late November 2016, a few weeks after the election that handed Donald

Trump the presidency, my three adult children and I snuck past the signs warning visitors not to enter the park after hours. My husband waited in the parked car, the headlights illuminating the parking lot as the rest of us scaled the gate, then headed into the fog. Using the flashlights on our cell phones, my kids and I navigated a short path, then emerged on the rock face.

Fierce wind rolled up the mountain and stung our faces. To get a full breath, we had to turn our backs to the wind. Huddled together, the cold seeping through our gloves, we tucked our hands in each other's elbows and surveyed the forest below. It was dusk, just before sunset, and everything below had a dull, grayish hue—the trees, the birds, the mountains. Normally, this state park received about seventy-nine inches of rain annually, but this fall had been one of the driest seasons of the century in our region, and now forest fires raged. In the waning daylight, we could see pockets of smoke here and there, a bit of haze in that valley, a mountain over there obscured by fog. The air smelled of campfires. The world was on fire, both literally and metaphorically, and though I could not yet know exactly how the next four years would play out, watching the blazes, I imagined the devastation in the woods—the terrified animals, the century-old trees exploding, the habitats destroyed, the stench of death—and I was filled with foreboding.

Then, just as we gathered near the protective rail at the rock's edge, the sun slid behind a mountain below, leaving only fire and shadow—reds and oranges and grays and deep blackness—a stunning display of flickering light. One mountain to the west was backlit with flames, a cinematic feat of nature. What had moments before struck me as tragic had been transformed, and the scene was breathtaking, otherworldly, spectacular. What should have been darkness was light, and what should have been light was darkness, and in that moment, I no longer knew who or what or where I was, from whence I had come or where I was going. Gazing at the blazing spectacle beneath me, I was air—cold, smoky, fiery, permeable, one with the vast expanse before me, part of the fire force that no longer felt malicious or destructive or a purveyor of impending doom but simply *was*. Light in the midst of darkness. Calm in the midst of chaos. Beauty even in destruction.

In his devastatingly beautiful book about the Vietnam War, *The Things They Carried*, Tim O'Brien writes about this inherent contradiction between beauty and destructive forces. War is "grotesque," he says, but also mesmerizing: "It's not pretty, exactly. It's astonishing. It fills the eye. It commands you. You hate it, yes, but your eyes do not. Like a killer forest fire, like cancer under a microscope, any battle or bombing raid or artillery barrage has the aesthetic purity of absolute moral indifference—a powerful, implacable beauty—and a true war story will tell the truth about this, though the truth is ugly." O'Brien's exploration of truth stuns me anew every time I read this passage. How does this knowledge of the moral indifference of beauty inform our lives? How does this change how we move in the world? Admittedly, beauty can be difficult to summon at times. In fact, as I write this, during a raging pandemic, following four years of political and social upheaval, just before the next election (which will most certainly determine the fate of this country), it almost eludes me now. Searching for it, I return again and again to the woods, and again and again, in every season, both literally and metaphorically, I find it there. In the spring, there are trilliums and mayapples and bluebirds and fawns. In the summer, gushing waterfalls and baby bears and patches of wild huckleberries and blueberries and blackberries. In the fall, acorns and chipmunks and buckeyes and brilliant fall colors. And in the winter, profound silences and solitude and miles-long vistas. Such exquisite abundance.

In her 1942 memoir *We Took to the Woods*, Louise Dickinson Rich writes about the power of nature to deflect our gaze from the hardness of this world, to shift our metaphorical tectonic plates. In the mid-1930s, Rich moves with her husband to the backwoods of Maine. During her stay there, Rich, who grew up "more or less a lady," has no modern conveniences—no running water, no plumbing, no electricity—and though summers in Maine are mild and lovely, winters are brutal. Early in the book, Rich describes the nightly trek to the outhouse: "This is no great hardship in the summer, but in winter, with the snow knee deep, the wind howling like a maniac up the river, and the thermometer crawling down to ten below zero, it is a supreme test of fortitude to leave the warmth of the fire and go plunging out into the cold, no matter how great the necessity." Even for 1942, this is a rough and rustic existence, a life well outside the mainstream, and thus the pulse, the momentum, of this narrative becomes threefold: Why is Rich here? How does she survive? And what lessons does she learn?

Rich, in fact, names the chapters after questions people have asked her—"Don't You Ever Get Bored?" "Aren't You Ever Frightened?" "Is It Worthwhile?" etc.—an interesting structural device that demonstrates she understands that her lifestyle is intriguing, even suspect, to the average person. In moving to the woods, Rich has become an "other," a feminine Thoreau. Throughout the book, Rich refers to everywhere other than the Maine wilderness as "The Outside."

The Outside is always capitalized, as if it is the proper name of a place, and this serves to remind readers that in Rich's mind, there are really only two places, her world and the rest of the world. However, Rich is no longer concerned with the Outside. It is what she finds on the Inside (my term, not hers) that interests her.

I first read Rich's book when a friend recommended it to me during our MFA program. A few years earlier, following a series of financial missteps, my husband and I had moved to a rundown, century-old cabin on fifty-three gorgeous, snake-infested wooded acres. Like Rich, I had grown up "more or less a lady," and the sudden shift from my previously complacent, comfortable life to one that involved more mice-catching and opossum-baiting than I had previously imagined possible left me reeling. During this time, Rich gave voice to my experiences in a way I was still unable to do. As I struggled with feeling lonely and isolated, I read about how Rich embraced the challenges of a life spent living close to nature. For Rich, hardship and beauty were one and the same, interwoven and intertwined, changing the narrator in myriad subtle ways.

Describing a winter day, Rich writes, "It was warm and sunny, and the ground was covered with a light fluff of snow, which was blue in the shadows, and gold in the sun, and faint rose and purple on the distant hills." The rich array of colors—blue, gold, rose, and purple—paints a vivid picture of a dynamic and lovely landscape. Again, later on, Rich describes a spot on the river beneath her home: "The river is deep blue and crisping white, and the cut ends of the pulp are like raw gold in the sun. All the senses come alive, even that strange rare sense that tells you, half a dozen times between birth and death—if you are lucky—that right now, right in this spot, you have fallen into the pattern of the universe." This sort of intensified sensory experience, this hyperawareness of sound and color, happens, in part, not in spite of the isolation in nature, but because of it. Her transformation comes when she is no longer of the Outside, and this change is gentle and understated, visible mainly through her quiet reflections on nature. "Looking back through the telescope of the last six years," Rich writes, "I can see myself as I was and realize how living here has changed me. I hope it has changed me for the better." Rich's life in the wilderness is one fraught with challenges, but it is also a lively, evocative testament to the transformative power of nature, one that is as intriguing as it is instructive. How do we learn to live our best lives? In what ways might we better meet the challenges of this moment? How and where might we find beauty during these unpredictable and fiery times?

These are questions I have pondered long and often since March 2020, when the Covid lockdowns began. In many ways, my family has been lucky during this metaphorical dead of winter. My husband and I have kept our jobs, and though our three adult children have suffered job losses and setbacks, we have all been healthy, and we have enjoyed many hours together we would not have otherwise. We have gone hiking and running. We have hosted family and friends for socially distanced gatherings outside. We have read books and watched all six seasons of *Schitt's Creek* and held, in our living room, a makeshift Banff Film Festival, complete with outdoors adventure films and nature-y snacks and free giveaways (*Here, take this Clif bar and these Smartwool socks I never wear!*). We have done more Peloton yoga sessions that I care to admit. Some evenings, we have lingered for hours over a simple meal, soup and homemade bread and wine.

Life has not been the same, and we have been constantly aware of the grief of others and the chaos happening in the outside world. Still, for us, out in this wooded hollow, we have existed on the Inside, so to speak, not untouched or unmoved but aware of our relatively good fortune, and it is in this quietness and familial solitude that I have begun to be aware of my own heightened sensory experiences. The thrum of a hummingbird's wings as I sit on the patio. The gush of the waterfall just after a storm. The first, hoarse crows of our rooster. The shift in the pitch as my hound dog bays first at a white squirrel and then at a deer and then— oh, my!—at a bear passing through.

Nature has taught me this. The woods have taught me this. Of course, the idea that communing with nature is good for the writerly mind is not a new idea, but it is a good one and worth repeating. In the wilderness, we find solitude. In solitude, we encounter the full breadth of human experience—death and destruction and hope and despair and beauty and ugliness, all of it at once—and therein lies the essence of a life fully lived and a story fully expressed. If you sit long enough and still enough and quietly enough, something beautiful will find you.

On November 13, 2016, five days after the election and a week or so before our family adventure at Caesars Head, my husband and I headed to Asheville to see Mavis Staples perform at the Orange Peel downtown. Smoke and haze hung in the air, and as the implications of the election began to sink in, we were increasingly despondent, both about the fires and about the undoing of our country as we had known it or, perhaps, as we had imagined it to be. As we left the parking garage and made our way up Biltmore Avenue, dread clung to my hair, my clothes. Everywhere I turned, I smelled the cloying, acrid scent. Inside the Orange Peel, I ordered a beer and stood in the back near the bar.

"I don't know how long it'll last," Mavis said to the audience, "but we're gonna make you feel good now."

And she was right. I had seen Mavis perform a couple of times before, and she had always been spectacular, but that night she was on fire. In a performance that was more tent revival than concert, more sermon than song, Mavis was powerful, majestic, true. *You're not alone,* she sang. *You're not alone.* And all the hippies and used-to-be hippies and hippie wannabes raised their glasses and drank and cried and cheered and sang and drank some more. Through her songs, Mavis gave voice to our collective sorrow, and something about her performance caught me by surprise, as if I had, in the five days prior, forgotten that such beauty existed. Even still, when I think of that time, of the fires, the election, the growing sense of despair, I think of it in tandem with that moment, of the way Mavis saw our pain, absorbed it, validated it, then sent it hurtling back to us in great, compassionate waves. We were not prepared to go there, but she took us there anyway, and we loved her for it, loved that she believed in beauty when we no longer did.

Since that night, when Mavis sang to a grieving, sold-out crowd about the change we have yet to see, I have had to work extra hard to root down, to seek beauty more and more often. *Look how the snapping turtles swim along the dock looking for handouts. Look at the red eft crossing the gravel road. See how amazing and strong he is, how determined.* Some days, I don't see it at all, except in hindsight. *Oh, look back there,* I say to myself days or weeks or months after the fact. *Look at that beautiful, moss-covered rock that was there all along.*

Perhaps it is a bit like training a hound puppy to sniff out a bear. I personally do not hunt bears, but I do have a couple of hound dogs, and they have the attention span of a flea, so I would imagine that it takes a bit of work to keep them on task. *No, not the squirrel. No, not the bunny or the snail or the pile of ants. Yes, that. The big, smelly thing. Good boy.* Perhaps, if I practice regularly, I can train myself to sniff out beauty more often. Perhaps, if I can learn to appreciate beauty more often, I will begin to believe there are beautiful things I cannot yet see. Perhaps, if I believe in beautiful things I cannot yet see, I might even be able to will them into being. Poet Ross Gay discusses a similar phenomenon in his book of brief, poetic essays titled *The Book of Delights.* For most days over the course of a year, Gay wrote about one simple thing that delighted him: a praying mantis, an odd turn of phrase, garden-fresh carrots, an airport encounter with a stranger, Mitch McConnell's smile/frown, of "someone whose penis is in a vise." In writing these essays, Gay suddenly finds his life to be, well, more delightful. In conjuring a thing, in tending it and cultivating it, his delight radar had grown more precise or perhaps larger, more encompassing.

When my thirty-one-year-old daughter, who had lost her job in Costa Rica due to Covid and had temporarily moved home, first told me about Gay's book, we debated at length over the distinction between joy and delight. Then, once we had agreed on a definition—joy refers more to a state of mind, we decided, whereas delight implies transience and surprise—we made it our habit to name a special delight we encountered each day. Some days were tough. In our small, quarantine bubble, each day felt much the same as the one before. More than once, when we came up empty at the end of the day, we even stayed up late just to see if something else might happen. Maybe the cat would curl up in the empty Hoka box that had been sitting on the coffee table for weeks. Maybe we would get a shout-out from one of the Peloton instructors. Maybe one of us would save the other one the last few bites of Jeni's gooey butter cake ice cream. Maybe the sixteen-year-old dog who shared our quarantine quarters wouldn't poop in her bed at exactly ten that night.

Eventually, we realized we had it all backward. Whereas we were staying up late waiting for a delight to run us down like a linebacker, we soon found a better approach. We learned that in order to rack up our tally of delights, we had to start early, so we woke up looking for our delight, and we did not let up until we had found something. My special coffee mug was actually clean. Butterflies flew in my daughter's shadow when she was running. A bear walked across the road in front of me on my way home from the store one day. Our new crested hen, Moira, laid her first egg (and, there, another delight—*Schitt's Creek!*). Before long, it was all we could talk about—this delightful thing, that delightful thing. It became a sort of competition, who could find one first, who was more delighted.

"You know," my friend Karen said when I told her what we were doing, "what you have found is a spiritual practice."

But, ever the religious skeptic, I was hesitant to label it as such.

"No," I said. "No way."

But Karen, who is a poet and knows much more about such things than I do, insisted that naming delight is a form of gratitude, which is, or so she says, akin to prayer. I suppose then that, using her reasoning, searching for beauty in the midst of mayhem, or at least being open to receiving it, is a form of prayer as well.

In the darkest, most hopeless moments of this past year, while I have sniffed out tiny delights to stave off despair, I have thought often of O'Brien's words, of artillery fire and cancer under the microscope and of savage, breathtaking wildfires charring great swaths of land. Before the 2016 drought was over, twenty wildfires had burned close to sixty thousand acres of western North Carolina forest land, a fact that amazes me even now as I ponder the devastation this pandemic has leashed on our world—all the lives lost, all the people trying to rebuild their lives in the midst of Covid, all the people whose lives can never be fully rebuilt. I do not find meaning in this destruction. I would not go that far. I see no silver lining, no lemonade to be made of lemons, whatever metaphor you want to use. But there are moments of staggering beauty in the midst of so much pain, and in those moments when life is hardest, I have come to believe that beauty and grace exist side by side, that in one we find the other, beauty with grace, grace with beauty. Still, when I consider how to move forward, I am often overwhelmed. Where do I begin? Where do *we* begin?

For me, as for Rich, the answer lies in the woods and on the page, where mystery and certainty, desolation and beauty live in harmony, where scorched forest floors give way to hillsides full of lady slippers, and wildfires morph into brilliant psychedelic displays. I may not be able to fix a single thing, to ease anyone's grief or abate anyone's fears, but perhaps if I keep showing up and doing the work of writing my truth on this page, you will see that you are no longer alone, and then you will write something I will read, and I will see that I am no longer alone. The destruction will not be less, you see. But we will be beautiful in spite of it.

THE THRILL OF DISCOVERY

Writing Your Way into Knowing

Though I am not an extreme adventurer by any means—I have not scaled high peaks during blizzards or jogged across the Sahara with only a CamelBak or commandeered a homemade raft down the Colorado River—the woods are where I am most comfortable, where I choose to be when I am lucky enough to have such a choice, and where I have cultivated the qualities that have served me best as both a writer and a human being: courage, perseverance, openness, resilience, fortitude. Normally, I am more content in the forest than I am anywhere else, but there have been moments—when I've almost stepped on a copperhead or a rattlesnake or when a fox or coyote has meandered too close for comfort or I've encountered a creepy man hiking solo on an otherwise deserted trail—that have left me weak-kneed and sweaty, ready to flee the forest for mainstream society and behave like the civilized person I know I am not. Still, I have, in my own way, embraced wildness. The years I have spent scrambling up mountains with my dogs and careening down trails on my bike have often left me feeling estranged from conventional life or, as Rich put it in her memoir, "woods queer"—queer in the old-school sense of the word—strange, set apart, unfit for civilized society.

At committee meetings and fancy wedding receptions and formal luncheons and teas, I am awkward, put off by niceties, bored by formalities and polite conversation. But in the woods, as in the writing life, there is no one correct method of going about things, no agenda, no one way to sit or one proper utensil to use. In the woods, as in writing, the detours you take, the moments where you stop to admire the turkey brush or the little brown jugs (I just looked them up and saw that their proper name is *Hexastylis arifolia*—who knew?), the moment when you sit on a mossy log by the river and eat trail mix and apple slices and imagine what might be—these moments become the point, the reason you return to the woods again and again. In the woods, as in writing, what makes you strange and aloof and unable to fit in the outside world is also what makes you unique and strong and capable ("weird but not wrong," as my son often says). In the woods, as in writing, the journey is filled with surprises. In the woods, as in writing, the place where you hide from the world is the place where you most often find yourself. The woods, for me, are where writing begins.

So hold the cucumber sandwiches and the Waldorf chicken salad, and drop me off at a trailhead with a dog or two or three or four and let me wander in the wilderness until I begin to hear the story humming beneath the surface of my life, until the quiet settles in my bones and soothes my clumsy, anxious spirit, until, finally, the words rise from somewhere deep within the forest and find me there, a story waiting to be told.

My first solo outdoors adventure took place not in the woods but on the two-lane road that ran past my childhood home in western North Carolina. In one direction, Country Club Road led past the high school to the funeral home that sat directly across from the only nursing home in town. It then ran all the way downtown to Main Street, where the big attractions were a drugstore with a soda fountain and a five-and-dime. In the other direction, the road meandered through horse farms and cow pastures and summer camps filled with kids from Atlanta and Florida.

It was 1969, and I was two years old. I was supposed to be napping, but sunlight poked through the side of the window curtains, casting long, spidery legs on the walls. How could anyone sleep with all that sunlight? Standing in my crib, I grabbed the bars and threw one leg onto the edge, ballerina-style. Then, with a couple of enthusiastic bounces, I sailed over the rail and onto the rug. Through the floor, I heard the muted slam of the dryer door, the rhythmic humming that followed. My mother was doing laundry in the basement.

I crept through the kitchen, past the open sliding glass door onto the patio. Outside, the stone was warm on my bare feet. It must have been Saturday because I somehow knew—I suppose I had been told—that my dad was playing tennis at the high school half a mile down the road. Easing off the porch onto the grass, then the driveway, I strained to see him there, but tall, skinny pines and massive oaks blocked my view. For no reason whatsoever, I suddenly desperately needed my father. I crept down the steep drive-way, paused, then took a right.

Though I often dream of this moment, of the field of Angus and goldenrod, the joe-pye weed growing higher than my head by the roadside, the bridge crossing the brown, gurgling French Broad River, I cannot say for certain that I actually remember any of this. We lived in the house on Country Club until I was seven years old, at which point we moved a couple of miles down the road, toward the summer camps, where I lived until I left home for college. Like all memories, this one is a hodgepodge of images, things I remember from that day, things I recall from the hundreds of other times I walked down that road, stories my parents told, photos from our family albums. Did any cars pass me? Did anyone notice a barefoot, towheaded two-year-old out power-walking alone? My guess is probably not. Surely a passerby would have stopped and picked up a toddler on such a mission, but who is to say for sure?

In any case, when I got to the slippery bank leading to the school parking lot—a small bank that must have looked like Mount Kilimanjaro to a two-year-old—I stumbled and landed on my belly. When I stood again, my hands were caked with mud, and a bright yellow-green smear, a grass stain, streaked the front of my yellow sundress. I started to cry, but then I heard the distinct thwop, pop, pop, pop-pop of a tennis ball. My father was wherever that sound was. Wiping my eyes with the back of my hand, I scaled the rest of the bank and stood on the paved parking lot, where I had a clear view of the tennis courts on the other side. And then I ran. I ran and ran and ran until I stood with my hands gripping the fence, my face shoved against the cold metal.

On the far side of the court, my dad bent over, his racquet raised in front of him, his legs springy. He didn't notice me at first, so I watched the ball volley back and forth until—ping!—it hit the fence, just above my head. And that's when he saw me.

"Jennifer," he said.

Maybe he screamed it. Maybe he whispered it. Or maybe he simply said it. In any case, he threw down his racket and sprinted toward me, a blur of tennis whites—shorts, polo, visor. Wisps of brown hair protruded from his tennis hat. His hazel eyes were wide. Outside the gate, he swept me into his arms.

"What are you doing here?" he asked.

With grubby fingers, I fidgeted with the white sweatband on his wrist. It was damp and prickly, like a washcloth.

"I wasn't sleepy," I said.

Then, out of nowhere, I was exhausted, and as my dad headed down the road with me flung over his shoulder, my body grew heavy, my vision dreamy. My very last recollection is of dozens of tennis balls scattered across the court, one creamy, lemony pool.

My memory fades here, and family stories take over. According to those versions, I was still soundly sleeping when my father handed me to my astounded mother, who had never even noticed my absence. She had put me in my crib, and she had assumed that I would stay there, which, I must say, is not a mistake she ever made again. I was not a child one could count on to be content and *stay put*, and from then on, if she wanted a nice, long break from me, she sent me to her parents' house, where I spent countless nights preventing my grandparents from getting a good night's rest. In short, from the beginning, I had a wandering and rather discontented and contrary soul, the kind of spirit well suited to the writing life.

In her groundbreaking craft book *If You Want to Write* (1938), Brenda Ueland speaks about the importance of writers wandering aimlessly, both literally and figuratively, and she encourages writers to spend time each day engaged in what she calls "moodling" or "long, inefficient, happy idling, dawdling, and puttering." This, she argues, fuels the imagination, and a strong, vivid imagination is essential to good writing. Moreover, tending one's creative power, she argues, is a sacred act. When I first read this, I was thrilled. The list of things I am inept at is staggering. I am terrible with math and ABC order and remembering passwords. I am rotten with financial planning, organizing my closet, keeping up with my car keys and my office keys and my cell phone and my Biltmore Estate annual pass. But idling? dawdling? puttering? At last, here was a concise list of all the things at which I excelled.

Thinking is writing. Walking is writing. Living your life is writing. Living a full life means that when you do put words to the page, what comes out will be something that matters both to you and to the larger world. Too often, writers fail to see this. They believe that, in order to be *real writers* (a term I have sometimes heard beginning writers use with a sort of perplexed earnestness that unnerves me), the task of writing must be all-consuming. But writers like this soon burn out—of energy, of ideas, of both. Writers of all levels would do best to avoid chastising themselves for time spent in other endeavors and, instead, focus on cultivating full, fulfilling lives. Enriching experiences will feed your work and your soul and give you energy to return to the task of writing.

To put this another way, say you are a distance runner, and you run sixty miles in three days but on the fourth day do weight training instead of running. Should you then say to yourself, *This is a waste of time. I should be running another twenty miles today instead?* Or should you see the weight training day as essential to your task as a runner? To be honest, I have been that obsessive runner who has a hard time doing anything other than running. For me, running brings a high like no other (even the regular, honest-to-God highs I experienced eons ago when I believed such things might be useful). I have been addicted to the endorphins, so addicted that I have run through injuries and illnesses and bad weather of all sorts. Once, I even ran through a tornado. Limbs crashed out of trees and landed on the trail in front of me. Dirt flew in my mouth and eyes. The wind almost knocked me down. But I had planned a run, and, by God, I was going to run. Now, however, I have more sense, and hopefully you do too. Hopefully you see the value of cross-training, of building the strong abs and powerful arms that are essential to your running performance.

Writing is just like that. Wandering, meandering is weight-lifting for your mind. It gives you the breaks you need so the story floating just beneath your consciousness can rise to the surface and make itself known. Here is the thing about dawdling and puttering, about strengthening one's muscles and piquing one's curiosity and teasing one's imagination: One trail intersects with another trail. One adventure leads to the next. One trail passes a deep, clear swimming hole. Another trail passes a waterfall. Another trail ends on a rock face with a glorious view. As it turns out, my little trek down Country Club Road was my gateway drug to new adventures. As only the best adventures do, it fueled my desire for more.

Five years after my tennis escapade, in 1974, my eleven-year-old brother decided that he and my grandfather would walk ten miles from my grandparents' home in Canton to Lake Junaluska in Waynesville for no reason other than that it seemed like a good way to spend a Saturday. My brother did his best to persuade me not to go because he worried I would slow them down, maybe even wimp out before we even got a good start. He wanted this to be a smooth operation, flawlessly executed, and in fairness to him, his concerns were not unfounded. By this time, the fortitude I had exhibited as a toddler was buried beneath several layers of anxiety, and I had a recent history of having major public meltdowns at the most inconvenient moments. But I had insisted, and, finally, my brother relented.

We headed out, down the hill, over the railroad tracks by the paper mill where my grandfather worked, across the Pigeon River, and onto the two-lane highway that led through Clyde to Waynesville. My brother and I wore short shorts, tube socks, and tennis shoes. My grandfather had no tennis shoes, no hiking shoes, only muddy boots that he wore in the garden and two pairs of dress shoes, one black, one brown. For our adventure, my grandfather wore what he always wore when he went out: navy slacks, a long, loose button-down, untucked, and his black dress shoes. It was a sweltering July day, and we had no water, no snacks, just an end goal in mind—the gas station next to the lake. There we would refuel on soda and snacks, then call my grandmother from a pay phone to report our mission complete. Though my parents frequently took my brother and me on short journeys in the national forest near our home, this was my first long adventure, and about five miles into our trek, I leaned against the cement barrier on the underpass of a bridge.

"I feel faint," I said.

Trucks whizzed past. The sun blazed down. I was weak and sweaty, my knees a gelatinous mass.

"You're such a baby," my brother said.

My grandfather eased down beside me. "She's all right," he said to my brother. "She just needs to rest a minute."

Eventually, my breathing slowed. The gray lines in my vision abated. My head stopped pounding.

"I think I can keep going," I said.

Before I could change my mind, my grandfather grabbed my hand and pulled me to my feet. Off we went, holding hands the whole way from Clyde to the lake. By the time we reached the gas station, I had a second wind—my very first exercise high. Despite myself, I had made it. I skipped into the store, pulled an orange Nehi from the cooler, popped it open on the built-in bottle opener, and chugged it while my grandfather paid.

"Can we walk back home too?" I asked.

But no one was having any of my nonsense. My grandmother was called, and we were retrieved. Still, it was a small victory for a girl who did not have a good estimation of her own abilities, and for the rest of his life, my grandfather told the story of that walk. He told it at Thanksgiving and Christmas and Easter, on my birthday and my brother's birthday and his birthday until it became a family legend, a tribute to my fortitude, my endurance, my stick-to-itiveness.

"Ten miles . . ." he would say. "Ten miles and you no bigger'n you were."

Of course, I had had a lot of help getting there. Nonetheless, what I knew about myself was upended that day in the best possible way. If I had not walked to the lake that day, my grandfather probably would have found another story to tell about me, some other way of telling me how strong and capable I was. He was just that kind of a man, and his recounting of that adventure says much more about him than it does about me. Still, in his version of this story, I was able to see myself as he saw me, someone stronger and tougher than I had previously believed myself to be, not a wimp after all but a seven-year-old badass, a tube-sock-wearing John Muir.

It was a powerful lesson in what would become a lifetime of lessons learned in the outdoors, and at some point I cannot exactly name, those lessons bled over into the rest of my life. You cannot do everything. You cannot be all things to all people. But both on the trail and in memoir writing, you can do more than you at first believe you can. You can surprise yourself. You can discover new things about your own life. You can come to understand yourself and the people you love in deeper, more complex ways. You can learn to take better care of yourself, to forgive yourself for all the wrong turns you have made. You can become more generous, more brave, more tender. You can learn to love better and harder.

You may be thinking, yeah, yeah, yeah. This is all well and good. But how does this translate to the page? What does this have to do with how to construct a solid sentence, how to hook one sentence onto another and then another until you have a paragraph and then a page and then perhaps the very beginning of a story? What does it have to do with plot and narrative arc and conflict and resolution and character development and so on? Well, nothing. And everything.

When I think I know the point of a story before I begin, the story loses its magic. But when I don't know why I want to write about picking blueberries or running a half-marathon

or assisting in the birth of a goat, when I am simply com-
pelled to tell the story, that is when the fun begins, which is,
after all, a perfectly good and underrated reason for doing
a thing—because it is fun. And if it is fun for you, or at
least interesting, compelling, an adventure on the page, I'm
willing to bet a growler of craft beer that it is going to be
meaningful for your readers as well. And it is this sense of
adventure, of living outside civilization with all its rules and
naysaying and easy definitions, that we writers must constantly cultivate. We must step outside of everything we have
ever heard about writing—*Yes, you may begin a sentence with the
word "because"! Yes, you may use a sentence fragment! Yes, you may toss
your outline!*—in order to discover new truths about our own
lives. This is the central task of the memoir writer: discovery. It is also, perhaps, one of the hardest things for many
writers to learn because we like to be in control. We like to
know where we are headed, and it is only when we embrace
the randomness of life that we truly become the best writers
(and humans) we can be.

Another case in point: One beautiful July morning in
2004, my husband, three kids, and I headed down the trail
to Hidden Lake Overlook in Glacier National Park. As we
began our hike, the skies were clear, the air warm with a gentle breeze. When we were about a mile down the meandering
trail, however, thick clouds rolled in. The temperature plum-
meted, and we were ensconced in a mist so thick we couldn't
see more than a foot in front of us. Turning back toward
the trailhead, we held on to one another as we inched along.
Then, in the distance, the mist began to take shape and
form. The figures grew more and more solid until we almost
slammed into two bighorn sheep standing in the trail. Wild
and woolly with tranquil eyes and grand, looping horns,

they rose from the mist like spirits. In our panic, our eyes wide, our hair soaked from the condensation of the fog, we must have appeared rather shocking. Still, the sheep calmly watched us watching them until, finally, the clouds began to part, revealing blue sky, and we navigated around them.

Writing memoir, for me, is like this: a backwoods stroll that, with one sudden shift in weather, becomes an adventure. Ueland argues that the process of writing—of dreaming and imagining—leads writers to higher truths, or what she calls "stretched understanding," a glimpse of the divine. And so it has been for me. I am not an outliner, a diagrammer, a Scrivenerer. I do not begin writing knowing where I will end up or even what I will discover along the way. I simply sit down and begin. Maybe I will write about the mouse I found in the goats' water bucket when I went down to the barn that morning, or maybe I will write about cheesemaking or training a new puppy, but, in any case, I rarely have any clear ideas about where my writing will go. I simply sit down and write, and eventually, if I sit there long enough, something will come. Or perhaps nothing will come, and I will have to sit there all afternoon until it is time for me to get up and take the dogs for a walk or make a pot of chili or whatever, in which case I will have to sit back down the next day and again the next day and again the next until finally the clouds begin to take on a certain shape and form, and I see what my story is becoming.

This happened to me often while I was working on my memoir *Flat Broke with Two Goats*, which was about losing my home to foreclosure and moving to a rustic cabin in the woods. When I began writing the book, I was still in my MFA program, and that semester I was working with Jacquelyn Mitchard, author of *The Deep End of the Ocean*, among other books. During that semester, I wrote a scene about a snake that fell from the overhang of our house.

In the scene, our family had just finished a picnic dinner on our patio, and we sipped on the last of a bottle of wine while the moon rose over the waterfall in our yard. When the snake fell, it dragged with it an entire nest of baby birds, and as the snake brushed my daughter's lap, the dead birds rolled across the stones between her legs. I thought this was a well-rendered scene, complete and entertaining in its own right. Jackie felt differently.

"Go deeper," she said several times, in several different ways.

Which, in retrospect, was just what one should expect from someone who wrote a book with the word *deep* in the title. Anyway, I went back and went deeper. I wrote about how my young adult daughter, who was terrified of snakes, cried so hard she could barely breathe and how she said to my mother, who was trying to comfort her, "This is the worst thing that has ever happened to me."

"No, honey. No, it's not," my mother responded.

There, I had gone deeper. Deeply satisfied with this revised scene, I returned it to Jackie, who, in turn, returned it to me.

"Go deeper," she said again.

And for a moment or maybe even a week, I thought she was being unreasonable, that she was asking me to squeeze blood from a turnip. There was nothing else there. It was what it was. And then, suddenly, sitting there at my computer trying a million different variations on that scene, it came to me: What my mother said was full of all the things she did not say, all the things she could not say, all the things brimming just below the surface of this moment. And so I added this paragraph:

She meant to be comforting, I suppose, but her meaning was unclear. Was it a lesson in relativity? Did she mean having a black snake and a nest of doomed baby birds fall on you wasn't that bad compared to, say, being stung by a swarm of bees or accosted by a mother bear? Did she mean worse things had happened and that someday, this incident would take its rightful place behind other unfortunate happenings? Or perhaps, was she looking ahead to all the shocking, painful things that were bound to happen in the future, things we had no control of, things we could not even see coming?

This line of reasoning then led me to consider how relatively minor the whole episode of losing our home had been, something I needed to consider both as a person and as a writer. Even before Jackie gave me the thumbs-up on this version of the story, I knew this was it, the excavation that revealed the true story, the heart of what had happened in that moment or, as Vivian Gornick put it in her wildly popular craft book *The Situation and the Story*, the "story" beneath the "situation." In the mist, I had discovered something extraordinary or it had discovered me, but in any case, there was a particular joy in that discovery which stays with me to this day.

You can write without discovery, of course. You can leave behind your inner explorer and bring, instead, your worst-ever writing assignment, the one where you had to write a five-paragraph essay that included a three-prong thesis statement and a conclusion in which you restated that same, contrived statement so that the readers who just read it four paragraphs before could, once again, revel in its dullness, its utter lack of originality. In other words, you can write to a scripted conclusion, and it will be easier. Maybe no one will even notice. But why on earth would you? Why, with as hard as it is to write anything, with all the time and love and grit you put into the creation of your art, would you settle for anything less than two stunning bighorn rams rising out of the mist?

IN THE WEEDS

Discovering Courage on the Page

On a beautifully clear, late-spring day, my daughter and I hiked to John Rock in the Pisgah National Forest near our home. The trail is roughly five miles. You begin at the Cat Gap trailhead near the Pisgah Center for Wildlife Education, then merge onto the Cat Gap bypass until you come to the sign indicating that the rock is ahead. This last, steep stretch requires careful maneuvering.

At the top, you reach 3,320 feet, and once you wander up and down a bit, you reach the rock itself, a 200-foot cliff with an ample rock face—plenty of room for sitting and taking in the view. From here, you can see the old fish hatchery below and the dirt road leading to Daniel Ridge and Cove Creek. You also have a spectacular view of Looking Glass Rock. At 3,969 feet, Looking Glass is a 390-million-year-old pluton, a popular destination for hikers and climbers. (A pluton, by the way, is a rock formed from magma that bubbled to the earth's surface and cooled before it could

become a volcano. Though I have hiked to Looking Glass
more times than I can possibly count, I just discovered that
while writing this, which goes to show you how many different ways there are of knowing a place.) When people emerge
on John Rock, they instinctively lower their voices. They
ease down in a dip in the surface, watch the hawks circling
below, the clouds drifting above. What I am saying is that
this is a sacred place, a holy place.

That day, the mountains were *springing* spectacularly. The
mountain laurel burst with pink and white blooms. Choke-
cherries sagged with fruit. Below, great swaths of emerald
streaked the kelly-green forest. Alex and I had settled into
two grooves in the rock face and were silently sipping water
near a woman who had swiftly and effortlessly passed us on
the last ascent. The power-hiker, probably in her mid- to
late forties, wore a band T-shirt, headphones, and athletic
shorts. Sitting crisscross applesauce, she sipped a beer and
ate potato chips. For a long time, the three of us sat there
together, the only sound the swooshing of bird wings.

After a while, however, a couple appeared in the tree line
behind us and began talking with the woman. At first, I was
annoyed by their conversation, but soon I was intrigued. The
woman was saying that when her marriage ended several years
ago, she hiked up to John Rock alone one evening and stayed
until nightfall before hiking down. Even in the daytime, the
trip back to the trailhead could be a bit dicey. You had to
make your way over roots and rocks, one poorly marked section where you might end up in someone's campsite if you
weren't careful, and multiple stream crossings before following the river back to the parking lot. But this woman was
unfazed by the prospect of bears and coyotes and snakes and
strange men, of holes to fall into and roots to trip over and

the myriad ways one might get turned around in the woods at night.

"I knew I was going to have to do all kinds of hard things," she said, "so I wanted to practice."

The woman went on to describe all the daring things she did after that night hike—rock climbing, solo hiking all over the world. Once, she had strapped herself to a strapping Marine and leapt from a plane into the Arizona desert.

"It was so beautiful," she said.

And joyful, I thought. *And radical. And bold. How radically, joyfully bold!* The experience of hiking out of a dark forest had forever changed her. By facing her fears, she had learned to believe in her own inner strength, to move through rejection and loss into the best new version of herself. She had learned to be joyful in spite of her divorce or, perhaps, because of it. In the hardest moment of her life, she had conjured something marvelous. Over the coming days, I thought of this woman's story again and again until I began to wonder: What if the opposite of fear was not courage, as I had always believed? What if, every now and then, you got to choose what to do with your fear, when to hold on to it and when to let it go? What if the path through fear sometimes led to joy?

Who is to say why some moments stick with you more than others, why some brief encounters change you in ways that are all out of proportion with the moment itself? I have thought of this moment countless times since that day. I have turned it over and over in my mind, examining it to see what it might mean, how I have been changed, and I keep coming back to this: I am not a naturally courageous person, but I have become braver and braver as I have gotten older. I do things I would never have done when I was in my twenties or even in my thirties. Courage, I now know, is like a finely tuned palate. It can be cultivated, coaxed into being.

When I was younger, I never ventured into the forest alone. I had internalized all the cautionary tales of the woods—Little Red Riding Hood and so on—but now I do a fair amount of solo hiking, and every time I step (or ride) onto a trail, I remind myself that I can choose to be fearful or I can choose not to be. The results of an encounter with the unknown will likely be the same regardless, so I try to choose bravery, to live the life I want to live, not recklessly but boldly, intentionally. Truth be told, I am much more afraid of *not* going into the woods than I am of being mauled or eaten there. I am afraid of becoming complacent, of living a life that does not inspire courage, a life that does not feed my soul. And so it has been with my writing life.

In his lyrical essay "The Way We Do Not Say What We Mean When We Say What We Say," Brian Doyle explores the myriad ways language falls short of conveying the complexity of human desires, motivations, and emotions "no matter how hard we try to mean what we say when we say what we think we mean." He then goes on to say, "Perhaps much of the reason we so often do not say what we mean to say is because we cannot; there is wild in us yet . . ." In Doyle's view, the journey itself is honorable. When we flounder around in imperfect language, trying but never quite getting things right, we are grasping for truth and meaning and purpose—in other words, the divine. The endeavor itself is holy. I try to remember this each time I sit down to write, each time I find my words failing to convey the breadth of my intentions and the depth of my emotions.

This idea was especially comforting to me in the weeks after my memoir was released. Many generous readers contacted me to tell me they liked the book, that they had had similar experiences to the ones I described. These messages were wonderfully reassuring and made me believe that my work mattered. Other readers, however, rejected the adage "If you don't have something nice to say, don't say anything at all," and my email inbox and my WordPress site contained a steady stream of messages from people who thought I was selfish, self-absorbed, entitled. I had anticipated some negativity. After all, my book detailed my family's financial troubles in great detail, and I knew that money was a sensitive topic, that some people would not be able to see past the poor decisions I confessed to in the book. I had anticipated that, although not everyone had made financial blunders, most people would relate to it on a more human level—as in, we're all human. None of us is perfect. We all make mistakes. Here is one woman's story of the mistakes she made and the reckoning that followed. Still, the venom people conveyed as they told me how much they disliked not only the book but me personally left me reeling.

"You might not have been so broke if you hadn't been drinking all that craft beer," one guy said.

"I can't believe she actually has a cell phone—how irresponsible," another person said.

"She's so whiny. I feel so bad for her husband," another guy said.

"Hopefully, she'll make some money off this book, so she can be more responsible and a better example for her children in the future."

And on and on and on. My "children" were twenty-three, twenty-five, and twenty-nine when my book was released, but through email and social media, people who might

otherwise have been thoughtful and empathetic felt free to
let loose whatever disparaging thing first came to their mind.
It came with the territory of memoir, and I knew I was one
of the lucky ones to have reached a point where people were
talking about my book in any way. Still, I was somewhat
disillusioned and unable to figure out how to move forward.

One of the hardest moments, however, came not through
social media but at a book club gathering I was invited to
join. I had attended one other book club hosted by a friend;
it had been a fabulous experience, and I naïvely had expected
this other club—in another town and hosted by a total
stranger—to be much the same. After all, they must have
enjoyed the book if they invited me to speak, right? I followed the directions I had been given to the hostess's home
and stood on the doorstep with a bottle of wine in hand. I
was the guest, but since the club met from five to eight p.m.,
I assumed this included dinner, and I was southern enough
to feel uncomfortable showing up empty-handed.

After I rang the bell several times, the hostess finally
opened the door, said hello, and walked back into the
kitchen. When she did not introduce herself or offer any
further instructions—such as where the other guests might
be—I introduced myself and offered her the wine.

"The host normally provides the wine," she said, taking
the bottle from my outstretched hand. "But that was sweet
of you, I guess."

In that moment, I understood that I was not a guest of
honor in the traditional sense. I was soon to learn that one
member had read my book and suggested having me attend
while the others had agreed without first reading my book.
When they (mostly) did read it, they had mixed reactions. I
found my own way out to the deck where there was a bowl

of nuts and some cheese and crackers, some wine, and a group of about eight women who may or may not have read my book. One woman who had read it was outright hostile, repeatedly citing her least favorite passage. For the most part, I sat quietly while the members debated the merits and demerits of the book, the wisdom or lack thereof of my life choices, and so on. A few members were gracious. A few were neutral. And a few saw this as the appropriate time to tell me what confused them and to give me hints for how to write better the next time. They asked me little, and I said little.

During this same time, my book was a featured read for OverDrive Books, an international digital library, and I received many comments—both positive and negative— from readers. The exposure was wonderful in many ways, and my book was read by many people who might otherwise never have seen it. However, the website had a discussion forum where people could discuss the book as they read. Some of the comments were deeply personal, and though my publisher had asked me to be part of the discussions, after a couple of days of weighing my comments carefully, of trying to encourage dialogue and discourage negativity, I was overwhelmed and had lost my good humor about any of it. Which is where I was that night at book club.

"Last semester, I took a course on Appalachian people," one of the women said.

Like all the other women here, she was from somewhere else—Canada, LA, Hawaii. I couldn't remember where. She was pleasant, well intended, but I couldn't quite get past the idea that she was talking about Appalachian people like we were an exotic species to be studied. Our behaviors. Our customs. Our odd little rituals.

"Huh," I said. "What did you learn?"

"Well, we learned that you all are very religious," she said. "And that family is very important to you."

It seemed beside the point to explain that, though I did like my family, I wasn't very religious in the traditional sense, so I simply nodded politely, which, I realize in retrospect, was a very Appalachian thing to do. In any case, the whole event was supremely awkward, but leaving suddenly might have been even more awkward and created a scene I did not want to have, so I sipped my wine—not the wine I had brought but the wine the hostess had provided—and when I could sneak out with some semblance of dignity, I did. I might have cried as I drove home, but I was too hungry, for one, and too shocked, for another. None of my own reading/research or the work I had done through my MFA program had prepared me for this, but I supposed I had learned a couple of hard but important lessons. One, not everyone who wants to talk about your book is a fan. And two, no matter how hard you try to tell your truth so that others will understand, you will sometimes fall short of that goal.

Publishing required thick skin, which I had thought I had before, but it turned out I had hippo skin, elephant skin, when I really needed the resilience of the tardigrade. Also known as water bears or moss piglets, tardigrades are eight-legged micro-animals that can withstand extremes in temperature, survive for years without water, and tolerate thousands of times more radiation exposure than other animals. They can survive low and high pressure and can even survive in outer space. The imperviousness and toughness of the tardigrade was what I needed when all I had was the soft outer shell of a writer.

Here is the truth about writing, particularly in the age of social media: You are going to have critics, and not all of them are going to be gentle. You can either let that stop you from ever writing another word, or you can buckle up and hang on for the ride. For me, after the publication of my book, this meant no longer reading negative reviews from strangers. It meant not engaging every time someone with ill will emailed me or posted on my website or tagged me in a disparaging tweet. Delete, ignore, disregard. This became my Holy Trinity. If someone had told me to be prepared for this, it would have been helpful, so I tell my memoir students to be prepared. You need to know what you may be up against so you can work on cultivating your tough outer shell.

In this same vein, writers must learn to adapt and respond to unpredictable, disappointing, and challenging circumstances. In writing, in working with agents and editors, in giving readings, and in hearing and, in some cases, responding to our critics, we need to know how to pivot and shift our energies to what is most helpful in that moment. Fortunately for me, my treeing walker Roo sets a terrific example in this regard, and she has taught me that courage comes in many forms. For example, she is terrified of the wire mesh covering a bridge on the North Slope Trail where we often run. Whenever we approach the bridge, she stops to gather herself, then darts across before the wire can trap her or eat her or attack her or do whatever she imagines it might do.

"Yah!" I tell her every time when we reach the other side.

And then I give her a treat because when courage comes, in whatever form, we need to celebrate it.

One day not long after we adopted her from the local shelter, I was out walking her in DuPont State Forest. We were on Conservation Road, a gravel road near the Lake Julia Spillway, when a man in a truck drove past us, then pulled over in the grass and stopped. He opened the driver's side door, then lowered his feet to the ground. Heavyset with a gray beard, he eyed me for a long moment before reaching into the truck bed. Though he was not overtly threatening, his silence was unnerving, and I was suddenly aware of how long it had been since I had last seen another person.

Perhaps I had read too many Flannery O'Connor stories. I pictured a gun in the truck bed—a shotgun, since he would have kept a pistol under his seat—but I reminded myself that since I had Roo, I was not alone, technically. I forced myself to keep walking—head up, shoulders back. I tugged on Roo's lead to keep her head facing forward, but, ever the social butterfly, she wagged and pulled and pulled and wagged, and by the time the man whipped out his fishing rod and tackle box, I had gotten myself so worked up that I had to look twice to be sure I had, indeed, seen correctly.

Still, it was unusual to see fishermen here and even more unusual to see fishermen who had driven there. Locals tended to fish in the Davidson River in the national forest rather than here, and, as a native myself, I quickly and intuitively cast him as one as well. The man stood with his fishing rod poised in the air and stared at me for a long time—long enough that I was once again completely creeped out. I kept moving. Roo and I were inches from him when he finally spoke.

"I like your dog," he said.

Both relieved and embarrassed, I laughed. The man had not been looking at me at all. He had been watching Roo.

"Thank you," I said. "She's pretty wild."

"Yep," he said. "They're like that."

I laughed some more. Ever since I had gotten Roo, everywhere I went, hunters and fishermen who might have otherwise ignored me struck up conversations about hounds: *Is that a treeing walker? Does she bay? Why are you running with that coon dog?* And then they told me their stories. Seeing a middle-aged woman wearing Birkenstocks and a Life Is Good T-shirt hop out of a black Mercedes, even a twenty-year-old, hand-me-down Mercedes, with a coon dog on a Gentle Leader leader, was a bit out of the ordinary. Roo did look longingly at pickup trucks when we passed them. She sat for long pats next to men with nets full of trout hanging from their belts, and once she befriended a young boy who explained to me how to teach a treeing walker to bear hunt. They are the smartest of the hound dogs, he told me. You get a bluetick, you might be training her for months, but a treeing walker will take right to it.

Truth be told, Roo had likely been destined for another kind of life—one where she wasn't contained in an invisible fence and walked on a leash but where she rode in the back of pickups and ran unencumbered on a bear trail for hours—and I might have felt bad for her that she was missing out if it weren't for her constant, unshakable cheerfulness, her dogged determination and bravery. Despite the fact that life had thrown her some curves, she did not worry that her current life did not precisely line up with the life for which she was bred. She improvised. In lieu of bears or raccoons or rabbits, she chased weed eaters and lawnmowers and mountain bikes. In the grocery store parking lot, she bayed enthusiastically and tirelessly at shopping carts. In our backyard, she overturned stones and howled at the insects she found. She dug up salamanders from the creek.

In short, she understood how to be happy where she was with what she had, how to make do and find her own joy.

That day at the spillway, Roo, in all her dogly wisdom, had intuitively understood what I had not: the fisherman and I were kindred spirits. Though poodles and bichon frises and Pomeranians and such were perfectly wonderful dogs, he and I were not poodle people. Poodles could be tamed. They could be trusted to walk off leash and ignore the two dozen eggs sitting on your kitchen counter. They would not tree your cat or bay at the armies of ants they uncovered in your herb garden. They belonged with refined, civilized people. The fisherman and I were hound people. We loved free-spirited dogs that spoke to our wayward souls. And perhaps, like the other locals I ran into on the trail, the fisherman had looked at Roo and seen in her another dog, a long-dead hound that had eaten the corners off his kitchen cabinets and run through the woods and slept on his front porch and wreaked havoc in his life the way Roo had wreaked havoc in mine. At least I would have liked to think so.

As Roo—or any other hound—can tell you, being joyful, radical, and bold takes practice. In writing, we cultivate boldness by refusing to skim the surfaces of our stories, by diving into the hard parts, the murky depths, again and again and again. Like a nighttime hiker or a pup on a scent, we hurtle directly into the things that scare us most. Sometimes I teach writing workshops about writing hard truths, and each time, I lead students through a series of writing prompts designed to get at tough material quickly. I ask them to describe the best things about their childhoods. I ask them to describe their greatest fears, their greatest regrets, the one thing they would most like to be forgiven for. I ask them to write about a time someone disappointed them and about a time when they disappointed someone else. I tell them that, in *This Is the Story of a Happy Marriage*, Ann Patchett says that the work of every writer can be "boiled down" to essentially one story, a story the writer reimagines and reconfigures throughout her writing life. In that spirit, I ask students what their one story is. And then, at the very end of this session, I always ask, "What is the one question you are most hoping I do not ask you?"

Usually, at this question, there are murmurs and sighs and *ah-ha*'s. The writers see the point. The point is going where you don't want to go, where you have previously been afraid to go, in hopes you might discover those things you did not know were hidden. The point is not necessarily writing about the worst thing you have ever experienced and sending it directly to the *New Yorker* (a mistake I made early in my writing life). The point is going into the dark woods even when you are afraid. The point is you may be far away from the life you had imagined but not so far from home.

COMING IN HOT

Zipping out of Your Comfort Zone

One spring day a few years ago, I found myself sitting, or sort of sitting, maybe more like leaning back, on a stool on a platform affixed to the top of a tree. I tried to appear relaxed, or at least as relaxed as one can be with a harness strapped around one's groin, but my legs were tingly, my hands completely numb from my death grip on the cable over my head. The death grip was unnecessary, as I was affixed to the cable overhead by not one but two different pulleys. Still, the phrase "hold on for dear life" came to mind, so that's what I was doing.

I had only met the rest of my group moments before. They were a jovial bunch—ten upbeat teachers who were enjoying this free tour as part of a special company promotion. Half the teachers were clustered around the tree trunk in the middle of this platform, half on the next one several hundred feet away. In other words, half of us had already made it to the next tree alive, which I took to be an encouraging sign. Our guide, Kate, stood at the edge of the platform.

Though my harness was clunky and clumsy, Kate's harness was cool and edgy in a Star Treky sort of way. All teeth and long, brown hair swaying in the breeze, she waved to me. We had been told to watch Kate carefully, and I took this instruction with the same degree of seriousness with which I took all safety instructions—fire escape routes in hotel rooms, emergency exits on subways, flotation device guidelines on airplanes. I focused on Kate as if my life depended on her, as if just by willing it, she could keep that cable from snapping and me plunging to my death on the forest floor below. I squatted lower and clutched the cable over my head, my gloved right hand quivering as I mentally recited the braking technique: *Press firmly, but not too firmly, on the top of the cable—flat palm, straight down. Not too hard. Not too soft. Even Steven.*

"You can do it," my fellow zipliners called to me from the other platform.

"Have fun!" the ones on my platform said.

Fun was not exactly the word that came to my mind. *Sheer terror* was more like it. This was all Jennifer's fault, by which I meant my friend Jennifer—*Other Jennifer*, as I called her, or O.J. for short. I had shown her the email I had gotten about the free ziplining offer, but she had been the one who was all gung ho about this adventure. She had quickly booked this tour that included not only zips but two rappels. As it turned out, the bumpy ride up the curvy, dirt mountain road to get to the start of the tour had been adventure enough for me. When the van driver finally pulled over to let us out, nearly backing off the ledge of the mountain in the process, I fairly leapt from the car.

"I'm good!" I told O.J. "That was plenty of fun for me."

"Oh, you," she said.

"I'm not kidding," I said.

But the van was already heading down the mountain, and she wasn't listening anyway. She was listening to Kate give an overview of what to expect. First, we would do a series of three short zips to get us acclimated, and if we did okay here on the bunny slope (so to speak), we could progress to the real zips. If we did not do okay here . . . well, she didn't want to mention that. It wasn't even worth mentioning. We were such a good group. It was already evident that we were going to be incredible zippers in no time.

But I knew what happened if you didn't do these zips properly. I had read about it when I was researching our visit. A woman had posted a review on a travel website complaining that her mother had failed the initial zip test, was not allowed to continue with the tour, and was not refunded her money. The company had then responded, and there was a rather heated exchange, which ended with the company essentially saying, Look, your mother could not operate the brake, and she was going to slam into a tree and die, so we couldn't let her continue.

I was like that mother. Though I had done a number of risky things in my life, I had done those things out of ignorance, not truly realizing the consequences. In reality, my list of fears and phobias was extensive: spiders, caves, elevators, subways, cruise ships, airplanes. It was not that I didn't ever go on a subway or an airplane. It just took a tremendous amount of resolve in order to do so. Resolve and bourbon or sometimes a small dose of Xanax. Now, I truly couldn't decide which was worse—dying on a zipline or being told, in front of all these people, that I was not going to have the *opportunity* to die on a zipline because I couldn't brake.

Unlike me, O.J. was not a worst-case-scenario sort of person. Moments before, she had gracefully and effortlessly slid down the zip and onto the next platform, and now she was kicked back in her harness waiting for me. It was now, I realized, a done deal. There was no turning back, no saying, "I'm so sorry, but I think I left something in my car" and casually slipping away. It was time to man up, so to speak. I took a deep breath, looked straight ahead, and jumped or, rather, stepped into space.

At first, it was thrilling, an amusement park ride, like the rope swing my dad hung on a tall pine in the woods outside our house when I was a kid. Trees whipped past. Sunlight flashed through the leaves. The next platform zoomed toward me. Kate smiled reassuringly. But then the wind picked up speed. Trees whizzed by at an alarming rate. Kate got closer and closer and closer. She threw her hand into the air like a crossing guard—BRAKE NOW.

I took a deep breath, let go of the cable with one hand, and reached over my head. As soon as I touched the cable, I swung sharply right. I readjusted my hand and banked left. I did all this while not taking my eyes off Kate, who was now mimicking the motion—flat hand, pressed down hard. I pressed harder, but it was too late. The platform was just ahead. Kate threw out the emergency brake. I slammed into it, then landed with a *thwop* on the platform. My companions cheered.

"Whoa!" Kate said. "You came in hot."

"That sounds good?" I ventured.

She shook her head. Apparently, it was not good.

"Did you notice you were turning?"

Did I notice I was turning? I was two hundred feet up in the air spinning around on a cable like a stoplight in a hurricane. So, yeah, I noticed.

"You're doing fine," Kate said. "We'll try it again."

But already I was flagged, flagged as a possible no-go, a middle-aged, feet-on-the-ground, no-braking mother. Everyone else had gotten high fives when they landed, and I had gotten a pep talk. I had two more zips to prove myself. Only two. The next round, I waited for Kate's signal and pressed on the cable with my palm so hard I could feel the heat from the friction of my glove against the metal. I still came in hot, but not quite steaming hot like before.

"Yah!" my new friends cheered once again when I reached the platform.

"That was better," Kate said.

There was one final training zip before the longer ones. This time I focused even harder than before, hand on cable, legs straight ahead, palm flat, breathe, breathe, breathe.

"You did it!" Kate said when I landed free and clear on the platform without the aid of an emergency brake. "Way to go!"

She high-fived me. Then a seventh-grade math teacher reached around the tree trunk to high-five me. Then a sixth-grade social studies teacher high-fived me. Then a high school chemistry teacher. I had passed. I was no longer someone's scared-to-brake mom. I was brave. I was power-ful. I had sailed solo across the Atlantic. I had scaled Kil-imanjaro wearing only flimsy shorts and a backpack. I had flown on an airplane without medication. Unfortunately, my moment of celebration was short-lived.

After a few more zips—slightly longer than the first three but still manageable—we got to the highest, longest zip of the day. This zip was more than 1,200 feet long and higher than the tallest building in downtown Asheville.

"Oh, my God," I said, staring into the abyss below.

"You'll be fine," O.J. said.

"Where is the other platform?"

"Over there."

She gestured into the woods. I squinted but could only see the vague outline of trees in the distance.

"You've got this!" Kate said before stepping nimbly off the platform. "See you on the other side!"

She tipped two fingers to her helmet—a send-off salute—before fading into the trees. She was Tinker Bell in a harness, and for all I knew, she had simply disappeared. One, two, three, four teachers eagerly lined up ahead of me. They flew nimbly out of the tree hooting like a bunch of Lost Boys, but when it was my turn, I stood frozen on the edge of the platform. All day, the sky had been overcast. Now, dark clouds gathered over the mountains in the distance. The tree swayed and groaned in the wind. I didn't want to stay here on the edge of a rickety platform on the edge of a rickety tree, but I didn't want to step off into the abyss either.

Moving ahead meant stepping into the unknown. This was a matter of trust. I could see that now. But I was a backseat driver, the one always double-checking to make sure it was safe to change lanes, to turn right on red. In that moment, I would have paid full price—$160—to climb down that platform. But there was no way down except by the cable, no way out that would not mean certain and profound humiliation. I had no choice. Or, rather, all the choices I had made up until this point had narrowed into this one choice.

"You can do it, Jennifer!" O.J. called.

"Try a cannonball," Kate had said. "That way you'll pick up speed."

Speed, apparently, was something we wanted here. The cable sloped upward at the end. If you braked too soon, you might not make it up to the platform. You might be stuck dangling in midair until one of the staff members zipped out to rescue you. This thought terrified me even more than the thought of falling. Falling would at least be over quickly. Dangling could go on forever. I waited, tried to summon courage. Time slowed. Or rather it swirled, one continuous loop, one moment in time. And there I was, seven years old, standing at the end of the high dive for the very first time. Gray lake water churned beneath me, and the air smelled of bass and pine. My bathing suit sagged, sending cool lake water dribbling between my thighs. I hugged my arms to my chest, rocked side to side.

"Go!" my friends screamed. "Go!"

But no matter how much I tried to imagine it all over, the warm wind rushing past, the sweet plunge into cool water, the cheers of my friends when I reached the surface victorious, I could not do it. Turning, I walked back down the diving board. At the ladder, I turned again, grasped the metal rails, then scooted down and hung in midair reaching for the highest rung. My belly rubbed the rough surface of the board. My hands shook so violently I was certain I would slip and fall anyway, die in disgrace on land rather than in water.

Though I did, in fact, make it down alive, even today I dream of that moment, that wild, frantic reaching which felt so much like cowardice, that set me apart from my friends who ran down the slide and did cannonballs at the end, from my brother who dove so gracefully, like a pelican diving for fish. But that was more than forty years ago. Now, I was in the last year of my first half-century on earth. There were still so many things I had not yet done, so many things I still wanted to do, things that required bravery and fortitude and a strong stomach. And though I understood that diving off a high dive or jumping off a platform didn't instantly make you brave, I also understood that this was a practice run for those other moments in life when actual bravery was required.

And so I took one long, deep breath and jumped, my knees pulled to my chest in the tightest, smoothest midair cannonball imaginable, my eyes wide open so I didn't miss a thing. Below me, the leaves were just beginning to turn colors—red, yellow, orange. I could make out a creek, wildflowers, a clearing of some kind. Next to me, hawks circled. And for just the smallest moment, I was no longer afraid. I was simply enchanted.

Getting out of your comfort zone is not something you must do only once in a blue moon. Challenging yourself, both in writing and in life, means constantly pushing the boundaries of what you believe you can do. Challenging for me may be different than challenging for you, but the point is to push yourself to try new things. I tend to forget to challenge myself. I tend to get complacent, to fall into easy routines. For breakfast each morning, I have yogurt and coffee—two coffees with one tablespoon of cream each, to be exact. I like to have exactly six quilts on my bed at all times, no matter the season. I wear only four brands of shoes. I am partial to eating ice cream a particular way. I line three cartons, all the same brand, on the counter, and then I get one or two tablespoons from each. If I want more, I go back through the lineup in the exact same order.

You get the point. I have created these rituals and routines because they are comforting and comfortable, but comfortable is not where I need to be as a writer. *Thrown for a loop. Out of sorts. Ill at ease.* This is where writers learn to soar.

So, go out on a limb and give a reading to a room full of strangers. Submit to your dream journal. Attend a conference or writing workshop even if no one else you know is going. Start your own blog or podcast or reading series. Apply to that ____ [insert fellowship, writing program, etc. here] that almost no one ever gets into. Apply for a grant to do research abroad. Write that quirky, weird thing that has been tugging at you but does not fit neatly into any category currently trending in agent wish lists. You will encounter rejection, of course, but what if even one person says yes? What if?

In memoir, we share some of our most intimate secrets with strangers: *Here is my past. Here are my mistakes, my fears, my insecurities, my deepest secrets, my greatest hopes for the future.* Perhaps fiction writers do not share this complex relationship with their readers. Perhaps the very nature of their craft allows them some distance. But I suspect this is not true. I suspect that every act of writing is a slow striptease that leaves us all vulnerable and exposed. I suspect that we are all afraid that if we leave the safety of what we know, we may seem hysterical, ridiculous, overly dramatic. Worse yet, we worry we will have no more stories, that we will never write anything good again, that no one else will ever believe in us again. Still, like that moment when you are poised on a zipline platform and cannot see the next one, you must summon your courage and take one terrifying leap into the writing life you deserve.

Perhaps you are braver than I am. Perhaps you have already ziplined through a tropical rain forest, and it was not at all scary. Perhaps you *enjoy* crossing icy mountaintops at night with bears prowling around you. Good for you. Now, push yourself further. Paddle the Amazon. Bungee jump off a cliff. Go deep-sea diving. Bike across Europe. Climb Meru.

Eat a vegetable you've never heard of. Mix things up, and do whatever makes your skin tingle, your eyes water, your legs tremble.

I promise you this: When you push yourself to new heights, both in writing and in life, you will become a better writer. The key is to find the places that scare you, then lean into the discomfort. Find a place in your writing where you have crept up to the edge of something hard and then walked away. Now, force yourself to stay there for a beat or two more, to sit with whatever scares you, to write your way through to the other side. In other words, take a deep breath and jump off that ledge into the abyss. Then hang on for dear life, until you see the world beneath you and hear the Lost Boys hollering from the trees. That's when you'll know you have made it out alive.

BACK IN THE SADDLE

Cultivating Resilience

My first real example of badass-ery as an adult did not come early or easily. After my reckless adventure down Country Club Road at age two, my own fortitude and wherewithal was something I had kept largely under wraps, hidden from others but mainly from myself, for the next forty-two years. And then, when I was forty-four, I purchased my first mountain bike—a black-and-white Fire Mountain Kona with front RockShox and disc brakes. It was the single most expensive thing I had ever bought on my own.

It is hard to say why I chose that point in my life, a life otherwise unmarred by broken bones or slipped discs or head injuries, a life spent strolling along paved roads or jogging down well-maintained trails, to go careening down Appalachian mountainsides over limbs and rocks, through branches and thickets and around hairpin turns. For most of my life, I had been a cautious person, a trait I had picked up from my father. As much as he loved the outdoors, he taught me a healthy respect for the dangers of the wilderness. He cautioned me about briars and bears, about strangers and venomous snakes and poison ivy. He also constantly reprimanded me for hiking with my hands in my pockets. You just never knew what might happen. You could trip over a root or rock and not be able to catch yourself. A twig could slap you in the eye. You could stumble off a cliff and into a raging river. You just never knew.

With that sort of upbringing, I never really expected to be in the market for a mountain bike. I believe the real reason I thought I could do a sport best suited for college kids was that I had been taking a spin class at the Y, and if you have ever done spin, then you know exactly what I mean when I say that doing spin makes you believe you can do anything. It's like cocaine. One line, and you are Lance Armstrong.

My first mountain-biking buddy—and you really need one of these to properly enjoy biking—was Meg. Meg had always been athletic. In school, she had played soccer and basketball, and she had been biking and running for years, so she agreed to take me on my first trail ride. Starting at the gravel parking area at Bent Creek in the Pisgah National Forest, we rode up the dirt road to Lake Powhatan, then circled the lake and turned up Hard Times trail, which was steep but wide and gravelly. I followed Meg as she turned down a steep bank.

"Stay low!" she called. "And sit back in the saddle!"

I gripped my handlebars and followed. We wound down the trail and came out on another gravel road. I gave a whoop, something that I thought might approximate what we did in spin after a good burst of speed. Perhaps I sounded more confident than I intended to, however, because Meg decided I was ready for a bigger challenge. We began winding and climbing. The dogwoods were in bloom, and from our vantage point, the petals looked like snow. When I got to the top, Meg was waiting on me. I gasped and wheezed. My calves burned, and my sweaty hands slipped on the handlebars.

"Try to control your breathing," she said.

This struck me as the single most ridiculous thing anyone had ever said, but I did not have enough oxygen to say this, so I simply nodded while she explained to me how to hit all obstacles at ninety degrees and keep my eyes trained on the trail a few feet in front of my bike. If I looked too far ahead, I wouldn't be prepared to navigate roots or rocks or fallen branches. If I looked too close to the bike's front wheel, I might lose my balance and crash into a nearby tree. I needed to focus exactly three feet in front of my bike at all times.

This sounds like a rather simple concept, but focusing was not my strong point, and I was worried I would forget where to look or be distracted by a squirrel or freaked out by a snake. Part of me wanted to cruise down the gravel road and forget the trail once and for all. And yet I had spent so much of my life being timid and afraid, and the list of times when this had served me well was very, very short. Perhaps it was time to try a new approach. Meg pulled an energy bar out of her pocket, broke it, and handed half to me. I gulped it down in one bite and threw back the last of my water. The trail in front of us went straight down. All I could see was the first rise of red dirt. I could hear my father. *Choose a long stick to roast your marshmallow. Don't swat at that bee. Keep your hands out of your pockets so you can catch yourself if you fall.*

"You'll be fine," she said. "Just don't stop, or you'll fall backward."

She took off ahead of me and scaled the first mogul in one lithe jump. Crouching low, I pedaled hard, gritted my teeth, and took a deep breath. *Focus on the trail in front of you,* I told myself. *Focus, focus, focus.* At the peak of the mogul, I rose from the saddle and rolled down the other side. I scooted back in the saddle and prepared for the next one. *Whoosh.* And again. And again. Five *whooshes.* I didn't have time to think of anything else, but if I had, I would have thought that it was like being seven again, learning to ride for the very first time. In a grassy field near our home, my dad had run behind me, holding the seat of my bike while I pedaled and pedaled and pedaled until, suddenly, a lightness took hold, and I was on my own. Only the wind on my face and the beautiful burning in my legs remained.

Now, Meg passed under a canopy of twisted trees ahead of me. She was smooth and graceful, and if I hadn't looked at the ground, I might have believed she was flying through the trees, a peregrine falcon or a Canada goose, and as I took a deep breath and headed down after her, I was a gosling learning to soar.

Mountain biking would teach me many lessons, but the lesson of where to fix my gaze was the first and hardest. *Do not look down. Do not look back or too far ahead. Look three feet in front of you at all times.* If you spend too much energy looking behind you or around you or too far ahead, you may lose sight of the very things you most need to see—the rocks and roots in your path, the tricky bend up ahead. You have to know where to set your sights, and you have to practice focusing until it becomes second nature, part of what you do whenever you saddle up to ride.

All my life, I have been easily distracted and even more easily overwhelmed, and this has been even more true during the pandemic. Over the past few years, everything I have written seems to fall short of capturing this moment in our nation's history—the political turmoil, the deep divisions in our culture, the violence and the threat of violence that looms seemingly everywhere, the isolation and grief and financial hardships wrought by Covid-19. There is so much to say, yet never before have I had so little to say, perhaps because nothing seems adequate to capture the magnitude of this moment.

Still, I try to remind myself that I do not have to say everything. I do not have to capture everyone's experience— and, in fact, cannot. I can only capture my own truth, what is in front of me just now. Sometimes, when writing seems most difficult, I start with something small and seemingly insignificant, something manageable. I try my hand at writing a piece of flash nonfiction. I revise an existing piece. I do some low-stakes brainstorming or journaling. Or I give myself permission to read something for pleasure or to reread a favorite book or poem. All of these things help me settle into the writing in a way that I sometimes cannot if I focus on the big picture too soon.

My poet friend Karen can attest to this "manageable chunks" approach to writing as well. After the death of her sister a few years ago, Karen wanted to write about her sister but was overwhelmed by the enormity of the task. How do you capture on the page the essence of someone you have loved so deeply? It feels impossible. Then, in a poetry workshop, Karen was asked to write about an object. Her sister had been a professional clown, and Karen instantly thought of her sister's clown shoes. The resulting poem led to another poem and another and another, and within a few months, Karen had completed *Grit*, a stirring tribute to her sister's life. Homing in on a small detail, focusing just on what was in front of her, had allowed a larger picture to emerge.

I used to think that the ability to pay attention was something one is born with, like blue eyes or red hair. Perhaps there is some truth in that. When my brother and I were kids, he spent hours doing word challenges in *Reader's Digest* and perusing the encyclopedia for interesting material. His favorite game was Monopoly, which I then considered—well, to be perfectly honest, which I *still* consider—a special form of torture. Monopoly required the things I was weakest at, such as sitting still for long periods of time. I struggled with these same issues all through school, and when I became an adult, I avoided situations, like formal meetings, that required my sustained attention.

What I did not realize then but what I have learned since is that while I might tend toward mental wandering more than some people, I can learn to focus better. I might always get antsy during committee meetings or have mild heart palpitations when asked to play board games, but I can improve my concentration for those moments that matter to me. I can learn to pay better attention, and I can use this skill to improve my writing life.

This does not mean that I write at the same time every day or that I have the discipline to close all the other tabs in my browser while I write. In fact, at this very moment, I have nineteen open tabs in my browser. Three of those are email accounts. Five are brunch reservations I began making yesterday and never completed. Two are news channels. One is Twitter. One is an Amazon order I began hours ago and have not yet completed. One is Spotify, which was playing last night when I went to bed but has now timed out. You get the picture.

Clearly, I still struggle with paying attention to the task in front of me, but I have learned enough about myself to take advantage of the times when I can focus. After a good hike or bike ride or run, for example. First thing in the morning. After a good dinner and glass of wine. Other times, when I know my creative mind will not be fully engaged (midafternoon, for example, or late at night), I save for editing, submitting, doing research.

Not everyone can write every day. Some of us have dogs to walk and goats to feed and eight a.m. freshman composition classes to teach. Daily writing just is not always possible or practical or even desirable. If you can write every day, do. If you can't, don't. Just be honest with yourself about what you can and cannot do. If you cannot raise your toddler septuplets while holding down two jobs and still find daily writing time, maybe just write on the weekends. But if you can't find daily writing time because you are too busy rearranging your closets or meeting your friends for lunch dates, perhaps it's time to reconsider your priorities.

Though not everyone can write daily, everyone can write *regularly*—whatever that means to you—and once you are writing regularly and well, you may want to set aside some time to look for places to send your work. Of course, you do not need to submit your work anywhere. You can write just for yourself or for your family, or you can self-publish or whatever you want to do. If you do want to submit your work to agents and/or traditional publishers, however, my advice is this: Do not do this during your scheduled writing time. Your writing time is sacred time, the time when magical, mystical things can happen, and the sooner you begin thinking of it as this, the better. Find a separate time, another day of the week or day of the month or whatever you feel you need so that your writing time remains just that—your creative time.

This has a dual purpose. One, you don't confuse time spent at your computer with time spent creating. Second, you create a separation between the disappointing (and inevitable) rejections to follow with the value of the work itself. Nothing is more discouraging than getting up the courage to hit "send" on a query you have spent hours or weeks or months crafting only to have a rejection email appear in your inbox only minutes after you have sent it.

Thanks, but this is not for me.

I thought I would like this better than I did.

The humor here is very understated, at best.

The editors have read your submission carefully; however . . .

And so on.

Once, very early in my writing life, a well-meaning colleague suggested that I keep all my rejection letters in a shoebox so I could learn to think of rejection as part of the process. This was back when old-school, mailed rejections were a thing, and let me say here and now that my colleague was dead wrong about this, and if you think this is a good idea, you are probably someone who saves all the hateful texts from your ex and periodically scrolls through them. Do not count your rejections. Log them, certainly, as you do with all your submissions (where you submitted, to whom, and on what date), but do not keep score. If you find yourself too caught up in your submission success rate, take a walk. Play a game of pickleball. Make a batch of bagels. Buy a new backpack or your tenth pair of running shoes. Paint your toenails or the bathroom walls. Do anything other than sort through your failures.

Here is what you need to do when you are feeling down-and-out: you need to be a mountain biker. You need to focus three feet in front of you, not so far ahead as to become overwhelmed, but also not so close as to lose your balance. Take note of any rejections that might be useful or instructive. Say to yourself, *Rejection is part of this life I have chosen. Rejection means I'm living the life of a writer.* Then tally your rejections in your submission log and move on. Head up. Eyes on the trail. Focus, focus, focus until suddenly it becomes part of your nature, until you are a gosling, and you and your bike are one with the wildness of the forest.

After that first ride with Meg, I was hooked on biking. It became my new obsession. I rode as often as I could with whomever I could convince, cajole, or bribe to go with me. I would drive. I would carry the bikes across the river. I would buy all the beer. (Meg and I used to measure the difficulty of our rides in terms of beer. "This is a thirty-two ouncer," we would say. Or "This is a forty-eight ouncer.") When you are in your forties, your list of potential female mountain biking partners is not as long as it might have been had you taken up this sport when you were in your twenties. It turns out that not everyone in their forties has time for a four-hour bike ride followed by two hours of beer and tacos. Nonetheless, for several years, I biked regularly with Meg and with my friend Margaret.

One morning, Margaret and I met for a ride at DuPont, a state forest located primarily on land that used to belong to DuPont Corporation. Years ago, this land had been heavily logged, and white pines had been planted to regenerate the forest, resulting in thick undergrowth. But long before that, before DuPont and Sterling Diagnostic Imaging bought the property, all this land, as far as we could see—more than ten thousand acres of trails, lakes, waterfalls, and streams—had belonged to the Cherokee. Now, gravel roads provided access to trails, lakes, and numerous waterfalls in the forest. It was a popular spot for hikers, horseback riders, and mountain bikers as well as for those tourists who pulled up to one of the parking lots, jumped out, walked a few feet to a waterfall, then hopped back in their cars.

The fog was still lifting off the field when I pulled into the Guion Farm access. Margaret stood next to her car, steadying her bike with one hand. She had just gotten home from a trip to Alaska, and she wore sunglasses, shorts over long leggings, two different patterns of knee socks, a multi-colored jersey that said "Alaska."

"*What* are you wearing?" I asked.

"Oh, these sunglasses?" she asked. "I got these at a Rockies game. Here, I got you some too."

"Oh, my God," I said. "How are we going to see the trail?"

"Just put them on," she said. "They'll keep the bugs out of your eyes."

I put on the glasses and dragged my bike out of my van. Then we snapped on our helmets and began to ride, side by side, across the dewy field. Next to the entrance to Hickory Mountain Road, a sign said "Danger! Do Not Enter!" We paused, then rode around the sign and headed down the gravel road, past the spot where rangers had cleared a wide swath of land. It was early in the morning, late in August, and the sun was visible just above the treetops. The air smelled of fresh-cut pine. Just past the old barn, we crossed onto the wooded trail that led to Ridgeline, a narrow dirt path that ambled down the mountainside through a series of dizzying switchbacks.

I paused for a moment at the top of the trail. It was a thing I did. If I had been the praying kind, it might have been a prayer, but really it was just a moment to breathe. And then I was off, careening down the mountainside, leaping over rocks and stones, leaning into curves.

"Don't look down," I remembered Meg saying. "Look in front of you."

I was one with the trail, part of the gentle, swishing breeze, the sun glinting through the trees, the squirrels scampering through the leaves.

"We're doing it!" Margaret called when we met at the foot of the trail. Her own blessing of sorts.

"How's the cabin coming?" she asked when we caught our breath.

My family was in the midst of the crisis I would later write about in *Flat Broke with Two Goats*. We had just moved to a one-hundred-year-old cabin on fifty-three wooded acres. The cabin was infested with mice and spiders and mold and mildew. The floors were rotting, the ceilings sagging, the water unfit for drinking, but at the time, we did not have a lot of other options. Eventually, I would come to love our new lives in the woods, but that day, I could not yet see how the move would transform our lives. I could not yet see the possibilities, only what was missing.

"Bad," I said.

"How's your mom?" I asked.

"Not good," she said.

She meant that her mother was dying, that she had just days to live. She took a sip from her CamelBak, I sipped from my water bottle, and together we stared silently into the woods. I had spent every waking minute for the past several weeks sorting through my children's things, painting, packing, trying to imagine what my life might look like a year from now and seeing nothing, just fuzzy gray lines on a dead television screen.

Behind us, there was a snort-huffing. We turned to see two horses, one white with brown, the other brown with a black mane. Their riders, a blond woman in breeches, a girl with waist-length brown hair, clucked and tightened the reins. The horses slowed and turned, then headed up the mountain. We watched them go, their shoes clanking on the rocks, two riders swaying on two ample flanks.

"Are you ready?" I asked Margaret when they were out of sight.

"You first," she said.

I led the way, past Lake Imaging and the picnic shelter, up one rocky, sandy mogul after another until we reached the crest of the hill. After a short reprieve, we were climbing again, to Conservation Road. Margaret and I had bought our bikes used from a local camp that sold their mountain bike fleet at the end of each season. When we first began riding, we could make it only halfway up this hill before we had to get off and push. Later, we learned to zigzag up the mountain to make it easier. But now we pedaled straight up, barely pausing at the top before turning left at the covered bridge at the top of Triple Falls, then crossing the wooden bridge at the Lake Julia Spillway. Joe-pye weed and Queen Anne's lace dotted the roads and the fields, and at the foot of the spillway were rows and rows of hardwood saplings with purple protective covers.

Any other day, any other time, the forest would have been filled with tourists at the covered bridge overlooking Triple Falls, on the quarter-mile trail heading out to the swimming hole at Hooker Falls, or at Bridal Veil Falls, where you could see the place where Katniss, her leg ablaze, leapt into the base of the falls in *The Hunger Games*. Cars and buses filled the parking lots and spilled onto the sides of the main road. Now it was midmorning, in the middle of the week. The summer tourists were mainly gone, the autumn tourists yet to arrive.

Margaret and I headed toward the old airstrip. Back in its heyday, DuPont had used the strip for business purposes, but now it was a novelty, a flat, paved strip on top of a mountain. At the end the runway peeled off into nothingness. Below was a valley filled with cornfields and pasture, and, in the distance, the curves of the Blue Ridge Parkway, the faintest outline of the tower on Mount Pisgah. Another morning, standing at the end of the runway, I had heard a rustling in the weeds and thought it was a snake, but then a turkey had emerged from the tall grass. And then another and another—five in all. I had watched them strut through the misty grass until finally they crossed over the hill.

Now, as we started up the mountain, Margaret fell behind me. I downshifted and forced myself to look ahead. Our friend April had been diagnosed with ovarian cancer four years before, and though she had completed one round of treatments before, she was once again in chemotherapy. Margaret and I, along with other friends, took turns driving her to and from doctor's appointments, sitting in the chemotherapy room and staring out at the birds circling the feeders while April slept in a leather chair, a blanket over her legs, a vial of liquid slowly dripping into the port in her chest. In recent months, she had stopped the shocked crying of the early days after her diagnosis and had moved to a state of resignation. CT scans, bloodwork, chemo treatments, physical therapy, and support groups were all part of our new normal. *A chronic illness*, April called it then. But we all knew better.

I pedaled harder up the mountain, through ruts in the road, past oaks and pines and maples. Soon this mountain would explode with color, but now everything was deep green, the morning air still filled with the stuffy heat of summer, the light filtering through the leaves. Halfway up, my calves began to burn, and sweat pooled in the small of my back and in the crevice of my chest. My breathing was ragged. The land sloped and evened out, then sloped again. I couldn't see the top of the mountain, but finally I could feel it as we climbed a pitch so steep that surely this had to be it, the final ascent.

At last, the light grew wider and brighter. The air was still and hush, the brilliant blue sky punctuated with mounds of white clouds that looked close enough to touch. To my left was a small log cabin where one of the park rangers lived. Green beans hung on a vine in the front yard, and a hammock was slung between two trees. I pedaled to a stop and waited.

"We're doing it!" Margaret called as she eased up beside me.

"We did it!" I said.

We crossed the runway and parked our bikes next to an open maintenance shed, then tossed off our helmets and sat on the ground. The pavement was warm against my bare calves. I tilted my head back in the sun.

"I brought raisins," Margaret said. "They're a little old, but they're still good."

I took one of the tiny red packs and peeled off the raisins that were stuck to the lid. A skink skittered out from under a tractor. We watched, riveted by his litheness and speed, by the flicker of his tiny blue tail. We were still staring at the spot where he disappeared under a corner of the shed when a man came over the ridge behind us and stopped a few feet away.

Of medium build, he wore a wide black hat over long black hair streaked with silver. In one hand he carried a yellow bucket. He stood with his back to us, his body pointing toward a cluster of trees in the distance. His stillness was palpable. Moments later, a woman emerged over the hill. She paused next to him.

"Look," he said to her, still not moving. "There she is."

The woman looked, and they were both silent for a moment, the only sound her rapid breaths.

"I knew she'd be here," she finally said.

"It's our deer," he said. "She's waiting for us."

I jumped up, my raisins spilling to the ground.

"Where?" I asked.

The woman pointed, and there, in the tall grass toward the end of the runway, stood a doe, slender and graceful, her tail a cloud rising from her body, her shiny, almond eyes fixed on the man. And, again, that heavy, watchful stillness.

"My God," I whispered.

Up until that moment, if you had asked me if I believed in an afterlife, in ghosts or spirits or ethereal visitations, I would have scoffed. And yet watching the doe's piercing gaze, I felt something—a pull, a tug, something magical and otherworldly. My voice must have conveyed some of that because the man, who had until this point been mainly shrouded by his hair and hat, turned toward me. His eyes were the color of onyx, sharp and tender, and there was something about it all—the man, the deer, the mountain— that unnerved me. For a moment, I could not speak, could not even breathe. I could not remember how I had gotten here or who I came with or where I was going after I left. Finally, the woman broke the silence.

"She's been with us the whole time we've been walking," she said. "She followed us from the minute we got on the trail."

Margaret was somewhere behind us, eating raisins or watching lizards, but not here, not with us, and we stood there, the four of us, me, the couple, and their deer. We were sipping from the same cup, drinking the same holy wine.

"Come on," the man finally said to his companion. "We'll meet her at the end of the trail."

The doe waited for the couple to cross the ridge, then slowly began making her way down the mountain, her path clearly parallel to theirs. I watched them go, the woman leaning into the man, the man a mere shadow against the sunlight, the deer a whisper in the pines.

"Are you ready to head back?" Margaret said.

I turned as she lifted her bike off the ground, snapped her helmet back into place. I wasn't ready to go. I wanted to lie on this ground and melt into the mountain, to crawl under the shed with that skink and ease into one of the solid, cool walls, to stay in this quiet place where no one was sick or dying or grieving, where the only sounds were the rustling of the leaves and the hawks calling from the treetops.

"Here," Margaret said, passing me my helmet.

"Did you see that?" I asked.

"Yeah," she said. "That was weird."

And just like that, we were gone, back down the mountainside, past the joe-pye weed and the Queen Anne's lace and the spillway and the hardwood saplings and the covered bridge, across Buck Forest Road and back to the field at Guion Farm where this was already a dream.

Mountain biking, you see, is more than an adrenaline-fueled sport for craft beer drinkers. Or at least it can be. If you do it long enough and hard enough, you will begin to build your stamina and hone your technique, and even though it will be exhausting and often messy and sometimes scary, you must stick with it because every now and then something strange and wonderful will happen, and you will spend the next ten years savoring that one quiet moment when, ever so briefly, on a mountain at the end of the earth, the veil between here and whatever else is out there was oh, so very thin.

Wonder. Awe. Mystery. Attention. Those are the keys to a creative life, and as writers, we must remain open to life's mysteries, to those things that we will never fully understand, to the deer who walk alongside us and the strangers we encounter and the places and people we love even though we will certainly lose them, to those moments that pierce our doubts and fill us with astonishment. Day in and day out, we're doing it.

Hallelujah!

Amen.

ECHOES IN THE MOUNTAINS

Honoring the Voices Within

Black Balsam in the Shining Rock Wilderness Area is one of my favorite hiking spots along the Blue Ridge Parkway. Though the crowds can be daunting during peak tourist times, in the off season, the mountain feels thousands of miles from anywhere, and the views are spectacular. At 6,040 feet above sea level, Tennent Mountain is the twenty-third highest peak in North Carolina. From the marker that indicates you have, in fact, arrived, hawks and peregrine falcons soar beside you. Deer wander the grassy balds below. The plaque is only a mile and a half from the parking area, but the climb up the rocks is steep, and on a blustery winter day, the wind is relentless.

As you stand next to the marker at the top, you must cup your hands around your mouth and scream in order to be heard. The chill seeps into your bones, and you must brace against the rocks to keep from pitching forward. Though it feels as if you are in the middle of nowhere, the parking area is only a mile and a half away. From there, the trail winds through an alpine forest and open meadows onto Black Balsam and then up the mountain. In 1925 and again in the early 1940s, fires destroyed the original forest. However, the resulting soil was immensely fertile, so now the balds, plentiful with shrubs and wildflowers, remain. On the other side of this mountain is a field frequented by campers and blueberry pickers, and beyond that field is Sam's Knob, the same height as Tennent Mountain, but the two-and-a-half-mile trail leading to the pinnacle makes the trip up less strenuous.

One January, my dad and I took my daughter, then in middle school, camping in the field beneath Sam's Knob. Wind barreled up the field so fiercely that I lay awake all night shivering. I do not know what the exact temperature was, but although we were dressed in layers of clothes and bundled in sleeping bags, I could not feel my extremities. At regular intervals, I woke my daughter to see if she was okay, a fact she still complains about today.

"I thought you were freezing to death," I say in my defense.

Perhaps I confused hypothermia with a concussion, but, in any case, I had likely read Jack London's "To Build a Fire" a few too many times. Adding to my sense of impending doom was the fact that we were eerily alone. We had passed few other cars on the forty-five-minute drive up to the parkway, and we had seen no one in the parking lot or on the trail on our way in. We set up camp in the sprawling field below Sam's Knob, and after a hastily prepared dinner of vegetarian hot dogs roasted over the fire, we crawled into our tent. All night long, the wind blew. Coyotes howled and screech owls screeched eerie, haunting sounds.

Truth be told, I didn't particularly enjoy camping. I liked the *idea* of it and all the activities I associated with it—hiking, biking, swimming. I liked the campfire, the roasted marsh-mallows, the way you sat in silence and stared at the flames long after the sun had dipped below the horizon. However, the reality of sleeping outside on hard, bumpy ground—the pollen in spring, the bugs and snakes and bears in summer, the dampness in fall, the bitter cold in winter—was not so pleasant.

I slept little that night, but when we crawled out of our tent the next morning, everything felt different. The sun had just risen, and the barren field glistened with frozen dew. Fog lifted off old Sam like he was pulling off a cap, and patches of blue sky emerged. Then, from very close by, came a thump, thump, thumping. A few hundred feet away, a pup tent had magically appeared during the night. Beside the tent was a camp chair and a set of portable speakers. A young man hovered over a cast-iron skillet on a fire. The thumping bass line blended with the smell of frying bacon and wafted down to our tent. Though our car was a short jaunt through the field away, I was inexplicably relieved by the presence of another human.

"Good morning!" I called.

My enthusiasm was uncharacteristic and, I would imagine, an unwelcome intrusion for this solitary camper. Nonethe-less, he waved a gloved hand in my direction, then turned his attention back to his breakfast while I stood marveling at this turn of events. While I had lain awake all night, think-ing about how isolated we were, going over and over in my mind how long it would take us to get to help if we needed it, someone had been right next to us all along.

This fact, that I have never truly been alone, has indeed been one of the great blessings of my life. Always, in the moments when I have most needed them, people have shown up to guide me—not always the people I have asked for, mind you, and not always in the ways I have expected—but, nonetheless, I have never been alone, even when I have believed myself to be. This has been no less true of my writing journey. From a young age, I was gifted with teachers and mentors whose voices reverberate through my consciousness. (Know the difference between a teacher and a mentor, my friend Karen tells me: Which one do you want or need at any given moment? Which one do you want to be at any given moment?) Even in those moments when I have been despondent and discouraged, when I have wondered why on earth I have chosen this life—or, perhaps, especially in those moments—I have heard, once again, those vital voices that have shaped who I am, both as a human being and as a writer. Perhaps you have these people in your life too—the elementary school teacher who tacked your poems to the classroom wall, the high school journalism teacher who thought you were funny and had a way with words, the college professor who wrote life-affirming words on your pages, the grad school mentor who pushed you to go beyond what you previously thought you could do, the person in your life now who tells you to keep on dreaming.

In 1973 my fourth-grade classroom was part of a learning experiment in which four classrooms with four different teachers were all contained in one giant, open rectangle—a "pod." My pod was dubbed "Camelot." The name was stenciled in brown letters next to an image of a castle over the entrance to our room. The mid-seventies marked, at least in my memory, the height of experiential education in the United States, and the pod concept was one where teachers shared learning strategies and rotated instruction according to their interests and abilities. After that time, learning became structured and standardized, but back then, we were all loosey-goosey and process-oriented, and the flexibility of this setup allowed me to grow in ways I can't imagine possible in today's outcome-based learning environments.

In any case, my language arts teacher that year, Miss Kempfer, was a poet who believed in radical notions like the value of regular outdoor time and daily poetry sessions. We read and memorized Wordsworth ("I wandered lonely as a cloud . . ."), Kilmer ("I think that I shall never see / a poem lovely as a tree"), Kipling ("If you can keep your head when all about you are losing theirs / and blaming it on you . . ."), Frost ("Two roads diverged in a yellow wood . . ."), and, because his home, Connemara, was just up the road from us in Flat Rock, Carl Sandburg ("If you ask your mother for one fried egg for breakfast and she gives you two fried eggs and you eat both of them, who is better in arithmetic, you or your mother?"). We reveled in the sounds, savored the joy and playfulness of the words. We wrote our own nature poems. We illustrated them, mounted them to construction paper, and Miss Kempfer tacked them to our makeshift walls. During that whole year, I never remember her uttering a word of criticism, not to me, not to anyone else in the class. Her comments were full of praise, marked by lengthy explorations of everything she loved about our work, an affirmation for all the ways we were learning to more fully appreciate the world around us.

That year, our entire pod—all one hundred children and four teachers—spent one day a week at a local camp where we caught salamanders in the creek and made corncakes over open fires and learned tragic Appalachian ballads like "Barbara Allen." Each afternoon, we paused to write in our journals and reflect on what we had discovered that day: a box turtle, a newt, a field of asters, a nest of tiny blue robin eggs.

Writing was how we processed our day, how we knew what was special and what we wanted to keep, and this practice of noticing and holding on to these details of the natural world stuck with me in the years to come and shaped the kind of writer I became. (The deep dive into Appalachian culture, accompanied by our twice-weekly clogging lessons, also served us students well in the coming years, as the region where we had been raised began to change rapidly, and huge hunks of our collective pasts became lost to us, and we to it. Unlike the generation of students who came after us, we knew and remembered from whence we came.)

In the coming years, I had a slew of teachers who were not at all memorable to me (nor I to them, I suppose), and then, in high school, when I was a terrible student and an angsty mess of a teenager, I joined the newspaper staff, which was, at the time, also a regular class. At first, I was a reporter, but soon, our teacher, Mr. Goins, appointed me as news section editor. I was not qualified for this position, even by high school newspaper standards. My grades in everything except English were terrible. I was not organized or responsible or even diplomatic. I was not a go-getter or even the slightest bit reliable. Usually, I was hungover, and I skipped so many days of typing class that year that I was almost not allowed to graduate. (Typing—imagine that! It is one of the most useful skills a person can have, and I did not have the discipline to learn it well.) But I had a certain degree of spunk, and I could write a decent story in a decent amount of time (snappy, edgy, hot-take editorials were both my specialty and my downfall), and though I generally brought more drama to the newsroom than any high school teacher makes enough money to deal with, Mr. Goins was endlessly patient and encouraging.

"Where you Goins?" my friend David and I used to ask him when we passed him in the hall.

Unfazed by our antics, Mr. Goins waved us away. We believed we were clever, and though he knew better, he never said so. At a time in my life when I rebelled against pretty much every other authority figure in my life, I liked and respected him, and for whatever reason—perhaps because he had a houseful of kids himself and an unshakable optimism—he knew how to motivate me to do my best. He ignored my bad behavior. He gave me hard assignments. He put me in charge of things. He paired me with other kids who did their homework. He expressed confidence in my ability to succeed.

The next year, my junior year, Mr. Goins appointed me senior editor, a position generally reserved for seniors. However, I would be graduating from high school a year early so that I could continue my shenanigans on the university level, so Mr. Goins deemed me qualified. It was a tremendous act of faith on his part, and for the first time in many years, at least as far as newspaper business was concerned, I tried to stay within reasonable limits, to shake up our little high school just enough without tearing it down, which, I came to believe, was the ultimate goal of the high school journalist. (I was, however, kicked out of my community jazzercise class for a humor piece I wrote, and I brought the wrath of the entire police force down on the paper when I ran a story about a car accident that involved the police chief's daughter. My transformation, you see, was not perfect—even in Mr. Goins's class.) All these years later, I can still conjure Mr. Goins in his slacks and powder-blue crewneck. He leans against his desk, a pipe resting in his teeth, his expression fixed precisely between amusement and astonishment, and it still stuns and humbles me to realize how much it mattered that this one teacher thought I was funny and capable and smart even when there was no real outward evidence of such.

Recently, I was running in the forest when I encountered a group of hikers. Because of Covid, I jumped to the side of the trail and pulled my bandanna over my nose and mouth. It was a chilly winter day, and I wore leggings, two jackets, and a baseball cap. With all my garb, I doubt my own husband would have been able to pick me out of a lineup.

"How are you doing, Jennifer?" one of the hikers, similarly attired, called to me as he passed.

Instantly, I knew his voice—not his face, which was obscured by a bandanna, but his voice. *Where are you Goins?* I almost called back, reflexively. But with all those other people around, it might have been awkward. And so I answered like the adult I am now supposed to be—*Good, and you?*

The voices of Mr. Goins and all my early teachers have not faded with time. If anything, they have become bolder, more insistent, and I carry their lessons with me both as a writer and as a teacher. *Notice the way the sunflowers pivot toward the sunlight. Look at the way the jack-in-the-pulpit bows toward the earth. Ask hard questions. Strengthen your lede.* And on and on and on. Life-giving, life-affirming voices. This is the wonderful thing about having great teachers. Their voices stay with you long after your time together, and if you have been lucky enough to have many such mentors, their voices join a chorus of voices guiding your work. Each time I comment on a student's work or lead a writing workshop or have an informal conversation with a writer friend or colleague, I remember this. I remember that what I say and how I say it matters. I remember that every time I genuinely encourage someone along their journey, I make a difference. (I am not talking here about insincere praise. I am talking about finding something in each work that I sincerely appreciate.) And I continue taking imperfect stabs at writing myself. As I have been typing these words, two rejections from literary journals have appeared in my email inbox. I have stopped, read the form rejections, noted them in the Google doc where I log such things, and carried on with my work. I refuse to let these voices rise over the others, the ones I hear even now as clearly as I hear the strains of "Barbara Allen" wafting from a lakefront mountain lodge.

Of course, your words are inadequate, these ethereal voices tell me. *Words are always inadequate.*

Write them anyway.

RALLYING YOUR PEOPLE (OR YOUR CANINES)

Creating a Writing Community

In the early years of our marriage, David and I acquired a slew of puppies, one about every other year. We didn't plan it that way. Still, about every other year, a puppy came our way. Perhaps this was the result of my naïveté or tunnel vision. Perhaps my nurturing instincts were on overdrive, or perhaps my puppy collecting was a testament to my impulsiveness and to my singleness of vision, my blindness and weakness and downright sappiness in the face of a beautiful puppy.

Back then, our house was perpetually loud and unruly, full of muddy paws, chewed table legs, and shredded blankets, but there was a sweetness to the chaos, a sense of fun and adventure. Our days revolved around playing and feeding and training, long walks and hikes in the woods, but by the time we were solidly situated in midlife, we had two young cats and four dogs ranging in age from eleven to fifteen and a half. We also raised chickens, dairy goats, and organic herbs and vegetables. After almost six years living in our cabin in the woods, we had finally taught our dogs not to run over the mountain to the highway or down to the plant nursery that shared our driveway. When they wanted to go outside or come in, they body-slammed one of the ancient wooden cabin doors until it gave way. Eventually, either David or I noticed that the house was filling with flies or crickets or yellow jackets and shut the door behind them.

For the most part, our days were quiet, restful, uncomplicated. A couple of days a week, I ventured into the world to teach. The rest of the time, I wrote and read my students' writing. David did his accounting job mostly from his home office. While we worked, the dogs lounged in states of semiconsciousness while the cats chased each other across their backs. At night, we fell asleep to the sound of the waterfall outside our front door and the peaceful snoring of our pack—a dachshund, a Lab/husky mix, a Carolina dog, and a beagle mix. Our dogs slept so soundly, in fact, that we sometimes had to shake them awake in the mornings. All creaky bones and dry mouths, they woke slowly, coaxing sore, arthritic limbs to catch up with their brains. Over time, the long walks we had once enjoyed petered into shorter walks, then leisurely strolls, before finally stopping altogether.

At times, I longed for a hiking companion, and people had told me that having a new puppy would make our elderly dogs feel more youthful, so when my daughter mentioned that she knew of a puppy in need of a good home, I wasn't totally opposed to the idea. The puppy was one in a litter of fourteen, all products of an illicit liaison between a purebred Lab and a sweet-talking, lowbrow wanderer from

Mississippi. All the puppies had to go. Or so Alex's story went. This puppy would be our spare tire, so to speak, our backup in case all our other dogs died at once, a bit of insurance against all-consuming grief.

The rescuer of the pups, Laura, had adopted two puppies herself. She then single-handedly found homes for all the others and arranged for their first set of shots and transportation to their new homes. On a steamy July morning, we met the transport driver at a rest stop just outside Knoxville, Tennessee. When the driver opened the back of the Fiat, I knew instantly which puppy was ours—the smaller, tricolor pup with tan markings just above her eyes—third eyes. Without ever looking back at her siblings, our puppy scooted into my arms and laid her head on my shoulder. At three months old, she was not a baby-baby. She was already almost too big to hold, and her huge feet draped over my arms. Still, her doelike eyes, her warm breath, her gentle huff-huffing were all very puppyish. I loved her instantly and unconditionally.

During those first weeks after we got her, Pippi—Pippi from Mississippi—was the ideal pet. She bonded quickly with our older dogs and quickly settled into our routines. In the morning, she patiently waited for me to put on my muck boots before we took our morning stroll to the barn. At night, she settled into her crate without complaint. And then, two days after my birthday and seven months after the publication of my memoir, I left to go on vacation. One week on a Portuguese island. One week soaking in thermal pools and eating queijadas and salted cod and recovering from turning fifty-one ("I'm *over* fifty now!" I kept saying with despair) and from all the hoopla that accompanies promoting a book. Sunday to Sunday.

When I got home, my sweet, docile puppy was transformed. She chewed my shoes while they were on my feet. She chewed the rug, the sofa, the vacuum cord, the phone cord. She gnawed on the dishwasher door, the kitchen chairs, the refrigerator door, the baby gates we used to keep the dogs separated at feeding time. When I tried to put my boots on in the morning, she yanked them from my hands and ran away. When we called her to come inside, she darted into the woods.

"That dog has got to be walked," I told David.

We had been waiting for her final round of shots before taking her on trails, so the moment we got the go-ahead from our vet, I loaded up her harness, a water bottle, a water bowl, a bag of treats, a couple of toys, and headed out. I was thrilled. Once again, I was going to have a walking companion, a dog who would enjoy long forays into the woods, a companion who would be as excited as I was about the prospect of a hike. I put Pippi in the dog hammock I had secured in the back of my car, then drove to the parking lot where we would begin. The trail I did most often was in the national forest. My usual route took me on a trail that ran between a forest campground and the Davidson River, then headed up a mountain a ways before spilling into the campground. I quickly put Pippi in her harness, leashed her, threw on my backpack, and . . . waited.

"Come on, girl," I said.

Pippi sat in the parking lot, tail tucked under, eyes averted. I coaxed. I pulled on the leash, gently at first, then more firmly. I stood a few feet away and held a treat in my extended hand.

"Let's go," I said.

She sunk her weight more firmly into her hips. Finally, I picked her up and cradled her on her back while I walked.

She tucked her face under my chin, breathed warm air onto my neck.

"We're going to have so much fun," I cooed. "There are so many good smells and so many animals, and you can go swimming in the river. You're going to love it."

She was quiet and still, and she seemed to be listening, so after a few hundred feet, I set her down.

"Okay," I said in a way that I hoped inspired confidence.

Without moving her body, she turned to look toward the parking lot we had just left. This went on for the next mile or so. I coaxed and she resisted, until finally I relented and carried her again. Even though everything about her was babyish, she already weighed thirty-five pounds, and I struggled to navigate the rooty trail while carrying her and my backpack, but I figured this was all a temporary situation and that she would soon get the idea of walking. She just needed more confidence. A few times, she walked a short distance after I set her down, and I was encouraged. Then she would see something that frightened her, and we would start the whole process over again. She loved people and other dogs, and she was happy to greet people when they stopped to see her. She just didn't like seeing them walking or running toward her, which was a problem since running and walking were what most people came here to do. I soon discovered that her list of fears also included

bikes/bikers
hats/caps of all kinds
fishing poles
inner tubes
children under the age of fourteen
low-flying planes

moving cars
leaf blowers
weed eaters
lawn mowers
air mattress pumps
trail signs

And so on and so forth.

I got it. I did. All my life I had been skittish, timid, easily alarmed. I had to work harder than most people to be brave, to push aside my worries and fears. I didn't like airplanes. Or elevators. Or subways. Or caves. Or wolf spiders. Or sudden, loud noises. I was a worst-case-scenario type of person. I exercised and meditated and drank straight bourbon (though not all at once), and still, I was overwhelmed by everyday activities that other people did without thinking. And so I tried to be patient with Pippi. I alternated gentle prodding with encouragement, which was not the slightest bit effective. Finally, I ended up carrying her over a mile until we got to the beginning of the North Slope, a trail that meanders around the campground. For whatever reason, something happened there. Tail up, nose down, she was the ideal hiking companion—confident, exuberant. She played in puddles, ate mud, rolled in the cool dirt in the banks, ran through the tall weeds.

"Good girl!" I said over and over.

She had it. Thank God. I was so relieved. How crazy would it be for me, of all people, to have a dog that didn't like to walk? Pippi was going to be my hiking partner, my companion on adventures now that all the other dogs were too old for such things. I was so glad we had figured this out. But then the trail spilled into the campground, where we had to navigate kids on bikes and older people in golf carts and college guys playing Frisbee in the grassy field and barking dogs and generators humming. Once again, she froze. Once again, I encouraged and cajoled and pulled. Eventually, exhausted, breathless, and sweaty, we made it back to the car.

"Wonderful job!" I said as I tucked her into the car hammock and fed her a treat.

I refused to be discouraged. Four-month-old human babies could not yet stand or even crawl, and even if we counted her age in dog years, she was still a toddler. Learning to walk might just take a little time. Plus, she had done well part of the time. It was a process, after all. Maybe a couple more walks. Or a few more. But before long, she was going to love walking. I just knew it.

Here is a spoiler alert: Pippi did not learn to walk right away, not for a very long time. The problem wasn't so much that she didn't like to walk. The problem, it turned out, was that she didn't like to walk with *me.* Or, perhaps more accurately, with *just me.* As long as anyone else—human or canine—walked with us, she did fine. On those occasions, she acted like a perfectly normal, not-freaked-out puppy. But the minute I tried to walk her by myself, my illusions of an ideal hiking buddy were shattered.

Her rescuer, Laura, had created an Instagram account featuring the dogs. It was fun to follow them, to see how the solid black pups with the curly-haired ears differed from the sleek-haired dogs, to watch them grow and change. One puppy, Tillman, appeared in a magazine ad for the University of Virginia. Others had gone to foster homes before moving to their forever homes. Gunnar. Libby. Bonnie. Baker.

Indie. Deuce. Stella. And so on. They had been together for longer than most litters, and I wondered if they missed one another, perhaps not in the way that you or I might miss a family member, but in some instinctive, primal way.

When Pippi refused to walk, was she remembering being taken from her first family—her canine family? Was she reliving the trauma of watching the siblings who first left the farm? Was she worried that I was going to leave her here? Or had she learned early on that there was safety in numbers, that as long as she was part of a pack, she was fine, but if she ventured out on her own, she was vulnerable? This latter theory was the one I tended to gravitate toward, especially as she attached to other dogs in the parking lot, to total strangers we spoke to in passing.

"Where are y'all headed?" I asked anyone who seemed to be headed in the same general direction we were. "Do you mind if we follow you a little way? She's scared to walk with just me."

I was the creepy dog lady, but I didn't care. I was so desperate that I had lost all sense of dignity and decorum.

"Pippi, come on!" I sang to the tune of Player's 1977 hit "Baby, Come Back."

I carried organic, human-grade (at least this is what the package said) chicken jerky everywhere—in my backpack, in the pockets of all my shorts and flannel shirts. On hot summer days, I smelled more like a chicken than our elderly hens did, but I suppose that was the point. My four-prong walking technique was this: I held a piece of jerky in my hand as I sang the Pippi song, lifted her by the harness, then moved her forward. Reluctantly, she inched ahead until, little by little, she learned that she *had* to go, which was different from *wanting* to go, but I supposed it would do. I walked her until my shoulder ached from the lifting and pulling, until the air vents in my shoes filled with dirt and tiny rocks, until Pippi herself actually started to look tired too.

"Yah!" I cheered wildly whenever she reached a milestone—the crest of a hill, the fork of a trail. "You did it!"

Pippi was amazing. I was amazing. *We* were amazing. I was a female Red Pollard, and she was a canine Seabiscuit. But the next day we would go out to walk, and Pippi would, once again, throw herself down at the trailhead and refuse to move, both literally and figuratively back at the beginning. I was sure Pippi had her reasons for not wanting to walk. I just wasn't sure I would ever know what those reasons were. I supposed it wasn't necessary to understand the behavior in order to correct it, but it mattered to me. Finally, David suggested obedience lessons, and though beginning training after having raised so many dogs was a bit embarrassing—a bit like going to Lamaze classes for your tenth baby—I was out of other ideas, so I agreed to try.

Six weeks later, Pippi had achieved her "Basic Dog Training" completion certificate, and she had learned some handy tricks like how to sit and roll over. However, I was still walk-drag-pulling her through the woods, and she had developed a new habit. Every time she wanted off the leash, she jumped up and bit my arms and wrists, leaving my torso bloody with what was perhaps puppy gusto but over which I had no control. Finally, exhausted and desperate, I did the most unreasonable, irrational thing a person with a challenging puppy could do: I checked the local animal shelter website for puppies. Somehow I intuited that Pippi needed a companion, a playmate, a dog peer who was not a hundred years older than she was. How would I like it if my only friends were 150 years old or even older? As I scrolled through the available pets, I found a litter of ten six-week-old mastiffs, two seven-month-old boxer mixes, and an eight- to nine-week-old treeing walker named Sue. A hound.

The website featured a series of three photos—two shots from a distance, one close-up. In each, Sue's neck was wrapped tourniquet-style with a bandanna. I suppose it was intended to make her look less *straylike* and more *petlike*, but, in reality, she appeared disembodied—a head with no body, a body with no head. She had the typical black, white, and brown markings of treeing walkers, but her legs were too long for her body. Wrinkles of extra skin gathered on her face, and a precious dark dimple dotted the bridge of her nose, just between her very-close-together eyes.

I emailed David a link to her photo, but he did not respond. Rather than being discouraged, I took this as a positive sign. He had not outright refused to consider the possibility. The next morning, a Saturday, I got an email from my department chair at the university where I was teaching two afternoons a week. She wanted to know if I might be willing to teach another section of first-year writing. If I agreed, that would bump my Tuesday/Thursday schedule from a seven-hour day to a thirteen-hour-day. I would have no time to walk Pippi on those days, and David would be at home with the other dogs anyway. We had a fenced yard. We were already doing all the things you do when you have a houseful of animals. What was one more dog to feed? One more to take outside? I mean, what could it possibly hurt to just *look*? By lunchtime, I had worked up the courage to ask David if he wanted to go see her.

"That's fucking insane," he said.

An hour later, I had convinced him.

"Just let me change my shoes," he said.

Which is how we ended up with Roo. The rain was torrential, the temperature hovering just above freezing, so we bundled in layers, threw a couple of old towels in the back seat of our car, and headed out. When we got to the shelter, the volunteer on duty said Sue had had two visitors the day before, and a woman from New Orleans had called about her that morning. The woman was supposed to call back with the payment later that afternoon, just as soon as she figured out how to use PayPal. *Allegedly.* Perhaps it was a sales tactic, but in any case, it worked. David went back to the boarding area with the volunteer to get Sue while I waited outside.

When David emerged with Sue, she ran wagging into my outstretched arms. David stood back, his arms crossed, but after three decades together, I knew this was a good sign. Though he was not exactly a send-a-dozen-roses kind of guy, he was a love-at-first-sight-or-not-at-all sort of guy. Therefore, having already fallen in love with Sue, he was now bored with the process, ready to finish the paperwork and get our puppy home. But that was not how this worked.

The volunteer ushered the three of us into the "Getting Acquainted" room, a beige, windowless space with two plastic chairs, a cheerful portrait of a young woman, and a portable rack containing leashes and other dog paraphernalia. Despite the painting, the overall vibe was *solitary confinement.* As Sue darted around chasing a pink, plastic ball, I threw off my down vest and sat on the hard tile, my legs extended. I expected Sue to crawl onto my lap, to cuddle and snuggle in an "I've been abandoned" sort of way. However, she was older than the website had said—three to five months old— and full of energy. She ran over, gave me a quick nudge with her freckled muzzle, then darted after the ball, which she chased nonstop for the next forty-five minutes.

In the photos the volunteer took of us that day, David and I look both haggard and starstruck. Sue is a furry blur, a coked-up hound in motion. Still, I knew instantly that Sue's easy confidence in her lovableness was the result of her essential *houndness* and would make her a cheerful and loyal companion for Pippi.

"We'll take her," we told the volunteer.

"Don't you want to spend some more time with her?" she asked.

But in our minds, it was already a done deal. The only things left to do were pay the shelter fee and determine the puppy's new name. Sue already knew her name, and it had a certain ring. *A dog named Sue.* Like Johnny Cash's "A Boy Named Sue," only with a dog. A girl dog. However, my mother's name was Sue, and though *I* would consider it a compliment to be named after a dog, I got that not everyone felt that way. But if we weren't going to call her Sue, we needed to call her something that sounded enough like Sue that she recognized it. Eventually, we settled on Roo, as in Kanga and Roo.

Roo, we were soon to discover, was just as mischievous as Pippi. Like the treeing walker she was, she spent as much time walking on her hind legs as she did on all fours. With Pippi's height and jumping capabilities and Roo's fierce determination, they were Thelma and Louise, hellbent on destruction. Even I, the Cleaner Upper of the Crime Scenes, could not fail to be impressed by their teamwork. Together, they left a truly impressive swath of destruction. They took the dishes out of the kitchen sink and rolled them around the floor. They gnawed the cord off my rice cooker and ate a box of earrings, backs included. They drank a few sips from a bottle of bike lube I left sitting out, cracked open a minibottle of Chardonnay and drank it, yanked open a bag of Asian slaw and ate everything but the sesame seeds, devoured two dozen raw eggs. They popped open a six-pack of Virgil's diet cream soda with their teeth, then watched the liquid spew across the floor. They ate the top of a muck boot, a container of feta cheese, an avocado, peel and all.

"Why the hell would you even want to eat an avocado peel?" I asked them.

When the dogs were tired, which they eventually were, Roo curled into a ball in the curve of Pippi's stomach. Once or twice, I even caught Roo rooting around Pippi's belly in search of milk. For some reason I did not fully understand, getting the puppy had reset Pippi. She now got that dogs were for play biting, and people were for hugging and cuddling. And, though you couldn't exactly say that she ever really seemed to *love* walking, she was emboldened by Roo's presence and eventually became a solid woodland companion. She had, at last, found another pack, one that made her bolder and braver than I had ever believed possible.

Now, let's be honest. Some of you people are poodle people. Or Pomeranian people or shih tzu people or the people of other tame, docile, perfectly nice, well-behaved dogs. You know who you are. And, really, who am I to try to convince you that you need to run out and rescue a wild mess of a dog that is going to eat all the newts and salamanders and crayfish in your creek, tree all the bears that pass through your yard, and terrorize all your white squirrels and raccoons and groundhogs? You have, after all, already made your choice. But I will say this: You need to figure out who your dogs—or people—are, and you need to surround yourself with those like-minded spirits who will give you strength and courage and, most of all, make your life more fun.

I know some people find this sort of community in their MFA program, and I did make a few good friends in my program. I am still in close contact with these people, and we have encouraged and supported each other since our program ended. I also found a brilliant and supportive community in a writing program offered through the university where I now teach. Still, this is not the only way to find community. There are many other ways. Attend a writing conference. Join a writing group. Attend readings at your library or local independent bookstore and introduce yourself to other writers and people who love good writing. Host a reading series on your own or with a friend.

However you do it, find two or three people whose work you genuinely admire and who genuinely admire your work, people who will be happy for your successes and whose successes will encourage and inspire you. Find someone with whom you are your best self, your most optimistic, most creative self. Then go adventuring together. Go skinny-dipping and search for salamanders. Run along a deserted trail. Growl at the wind. Bark wildly at the birds. Do something, anything, to get out of the rut you are in.

Then when you are finished exploring, get back inside and shake up your writing. If you always write to prompts, freewrite this time, about anything—what you dreamed last night, what you had for dinner, what you smelled when you were out trail running. If you never use prompts, go to the website for *Poets & Writers* and use one of the prompts they suggest, or write about one of the questions at the end of this book. If you always write on your laptop, write in a notebook, or vice versa. Make a playlist of songs that inspire you, and play it while you work. Find an old story you have written. Take one paragraph that you love, put it at the top of a new document, and start from there, writing a totally new piece. Take a fiction piece and make it nonfiction or vice versa. Make a story into a video essay. Transform a poem into a song. Take a 4,000-word essay, and cut and distill and distill and cut until you have 800 words of flash nonfiction. Take a piece of flash and expand it into a short story. Copy a sentence from your favorite book and make it your own by replacing each part of speech with another word that is the same part of speech until you have your own, unique sentence.

Then—and this is the hard part—share it with someone. Send it to someone in your writing group or a friend whose opinion you trust or take it to an open-mic night at your local library or bookstore or café or stand in your living room and read it aloud to your treeing walker or your Lab or maybe all six of your dogs because they have been on this writing journey with you all along, and they are gigantic furballs of encouragement and positivity, and who doesn't need more of that in their writing life?

The point is, in sharing your work, you join the mighty, messy community of writers who will help you resee your work in meaningful ways. And by occasionally mixing up your writing routine, you create new pathways, new ways to access material that may be stubbornly lodged somewhere between your brain and the page. My daughter once read somewhere that you should always walk new routes because walking in new places causes you to think new thoughts. Not being scientifically inclined, I have no idea if this is real science or pseudoscience, but for me this often works.

In order to be the best writer and human I can be, I have to channel my inner hound dog. I have to lead with my nose to the ground, curious and open to whatever comes my way. A squirrel? Awesome! A deer in rut? Even better! A bear cub crossing the path in front of me?

Jackpot.

A LIGHTER LOAD

Unpacking the Writing Life

At 6,593 feet, Mount LeConte in the Great Smoky Mountains National Park in Tennessee is the third largest mountain in the Smokies and is not accessible by road. From the forest entrances near Gatlinburg, visitors can take one of five trails—Alum Cave, Boulevard, Bullhead, Rainbow Falls, or Trillium Gap. The trails are varying lengths and grades, but all are steep and rocky. The views along the way and at the summit are spectacular, and at the top there are cabins, a lodge, a few outdoor bathrooms, and a dining hall, all operated by the U.S. Forest Service. Once a week, llamas pack in food and other necessities to keep the dining hall and other facilities running smoothly.

When my kids were little, I was part of a group of women who had a standing reservation at one of the cabins the first Thursday in April each year. New reservations later became very hard to get, but somehow we were grandfathered in for that date, and though the group changed a bit from year to year and we eventually lost our special standing, for a number of years we made the annual trek. One spring sometime in the late nineties, seven women donned our best zip-off pants and boots, stuffed our backpacks with bars of chocolate and bottles of wine, and carpooled to the Trillium Gap trailhead (so named for the clusters of trilliums that covered the hillsides). Our plan was to hike in, eat dinner in the lodge, spend the night in one of the cabins at the top, and hike back down the next morning.

By the time we got to the trailhead, the misty rain that had begun earlier that morning became a hard, driving rain. But we were here. We had arranged for days off work. We had shipped our kids off to their grandparents or other friends. We had been training extra hard on the trails at home and at the gym. Plus, we had made our cabin reservation more than a year before, and it could not be changed, so we threw on ponchos over our clothes and backpacks and headed out. Trillium Gap is six and a half miles long with 3,300 feet of climbing, and as we climbed higher, the mountain became ensconced in thick fog. Only able to see a few feet in front of us, we hiked single file. Then the rain turned to sleet. And then it turned to snow. Finally, the terrain leveled, and through the murky distance, the lodge appeared. In our cabin, a rustic, sparse three-room affair with eight beds and a small gas stove, we shed our wet clothes and hung them over railings and bedposts. Then, dressed in all the remaining clothes in our packs—our sleeping clothes and our clean hiking clothes—we headed to the lodge.

The dining room was warm and full of hikers exchanging stories from the trail. We drank the complimentary hot chocolate, then sat at one of the long wooden tables and waited to be served. We knew what was coming, yet each time we were still surprised that the lodge produced such a spread from canned and dry goods packed in by llamas. The menu was always the same—canned meat, boxed mashed potatoes, applesauce, half a canned peach, a chocolate chip cookie. We lingered over our meal as long as we could, then headed directly to our cabin and dove into bed with all our clothes still on.

The cabin was heated only by a small gas stove, and in addition to my leggings, shirt, and jacket, I slept in gloves, a hat, neck warmer wrapped around my face. By the luck of the draw, I had ended up in a top bunk that I had thought would be warmer, but the one exposed area of my body—my nose—was so cold I kept waking up. Finally, I remembered I had a Band-Aid in my jacket pocket. Once I had managed to cover the tip of my nose, I finally fell asleep. At two a.m., however, I woke to the sound of wind screaming through the cabin and a burning in my abdomen: I had to pee. With much effort, I made my way down from the top bunk. Shining my flashlight, I found my boots and was just slipping them on when my longtime friend Ann called to me from her bunk.

"Where are you going?"

"I have to pee."

"With the bear outside?"

"What bear?"

Silently, she parted the window curtain next to her bed. Just outside, a large black bear paced back and forth in the moonlight. The fancy-for-an-outhouse outhouse was a few hundred feet from our cabin. Getting there required navigating icy rocks in near total darkness. With a bear pacing nervously outside. Nonetheless, I had to pee, and we had no plan for peeing indoors.

"You have to come with me," I told Ann.

"Oh, no," she said. "I'm not going out there."

But I was insistent, alternately begging and badgering, until, finally, she donned her boots and gloves. We grabbed headlamps and flashlights, one each for each of us, and headed outside. As many times as I have been told what to do when you encounter a bear in the wilderness, in the times when I have needed this information, I have always forgotten the specifics. Do you get big and loud? Do you back quietly away? Do you fall on the ground and play dead? One of these responses is recommended for an encounter with a wild cat, I think, which is not really an issue around here. Also, I think one is better for a black bear and another for a grizzly, which we don't have around here either, but in the moment, none of this was too clear, so as Ann and I trekked through the howling winds and over the ice to the outhouse, I furiously clapped my gloved hands and hollered, "Go away, bear!"

"What good is that going to do?" she asked.

I wasn't sure, but yelling made me feel better. At the out-house, she stood outside on bear duty while I propped my flashlight on the sink for light, pulled down my two pairs of pants and long underwear and then regular underwear, and peed.

"Come on," Ann kept saying. "Hurry up!"

Finally, my bladder relieved and my clothes back on, I grabbed my phone and stumbled outside. Ann and I linked arms and walked-ran back to our cabin. Her last words before I headed back to my bunk were, "You owe me one." Her act of bravery was, of course, noteworthy, but for the next decade, she milked it for all it was worth. Whenever she needed a favor, and I hesitated, she would say, "Remember that time . . ." Now, she doesn't even have to say it. She will just look at me a certain way, and I will see it in her eyes.

"Okay, okay," I say. "I'll do it."

The morning after we saw the bear, we woke to a foot or so of snow, the treacherous, ice-glazed kind of snow. We didn't bother changing clothes. We just pulled more clothes on over our pajamas, and, after a quick breakfast in the dining hall, we loaded our packs and headed down the mountain. We had planned to descend along Alum Cave Trail, which is normally spectacularly beautiful. The cave is worth the trip itself, but there are also many incredible views toward the top as the trail narrows and even, at times, disappears into sheer rock. We clung to cables as we shimmied down steep, open rock faces in breathtaking wind. The trek was arduous and slow, but when we reached the parking lot a few hours later, we were elated, ecstatic. Our athleticism and fortitude and adventurous spirits were boundless. We were Sir Edmund Hillary, George Mallory, Junko Tabei.

Over the years, I have hiked all the trails at LeConte, some several times, all at the same time of year, and one of the most challenging parts of the entire endeavor has been learning to pack properly. It could be spring at the trailhead and winter at the top, or it could be blazing hot the whole way. You might hike through ice and snow or torrential rain or, as we did that one year, all three in the same day, so you have to plan for all contingencies—to pack everything you might possibly need but not so much that your pack is too heavy to carry up the mountain.

My older son was a camp director for a while, and he is a fabulous packer. At any given moment on any given trail, he will whip out some new, vital thing: a rain poncho, dry socks, an extra pullover, extra water, energy bars, tools of all kinds, a solar charger, Moleskin, sunscreen, Band-Aids, splints and bandages and medical tape, medicines for stomach cramps and headaches and burns and bug bites and bee stings. The list goes on. I, however, sometimes have a hard time determining what is necessary on any given trek. How many sandwiches will I need? How many Snickers bars? How many pairs of pants? Should I take a second pair of shoes? What about a pillow? Once a woman I knew carried two full bottles of wine and ingredients for a full charcuterie board all the way to the LeConte summit. I, myself, have been known to pack in a couple (okay, up to ten but no more than that) single-serving wine bottles. Some people might consider that unnecessary, but it depends on what you mean by *necessary*. Am I going to need to pee in an outhouse in subzero temperatures with a bear wandering around outside? If so, wine is most definitely necessary.

The year my friend April hiked Mount LeConte, I wasn't able to go, but she told me the story of that day so many times afterward I sometimes have to remind myself I wasn't there. That year, the other hikers were all distance runners and hikers who could easily run the trail up and back in a few hours. However, they planned to stay overnight at the top. April liked the *idea* of hiking. She liked the gear—the Smartwool socks and Merrell boots, the North Face pants, the Patagonia backpack, the moisture-wicking Columbia top with built-in sunscreen—and she liked the camaraderie of the all-women adventure. However, she was out of shape, and she had overpacked. In her pack, she carried lunch and snacks and wine, a pair of flannel pajamas, a fluffy towel, a robe and slippers, a change of clothes, sunscreen, bug spray, makeup, toiletries. Though she began hiking at a reasonable pace, she soon fell behind the rest of the group. By the time she approached the summit, she was exhausted, spent, barely moving—and completely alone. That was when she noticed buzzards swarming overheard.

"I knew I was going slow," she later told me. "But I didn't know I was going *that* slow."

When she finally stumbled into the cabin, her fellow hikers were just preparing to search for her. For years afterward, she recalled this as the singular most horrible outdoors experience of her life, and she vowed that if she ever hiked LeConte again, she would take only a toothbrush and a bag of marshmallows. In other words, she would carry a lighter load.

Amen to that. Amen. May we all carry lighter loads.

Like hikers, writers need to come to their task prepared for dramatic shifts in conditions. The field of writing is packed and ever changing, and trends in publishing come and go, but there are some basics elements of craft every writer needs to know, basics you can discover by doing your homework and reading a wide variety of works. This seems like a no-brainer, but because we sometimes forget the easy, obvious things like the rain poncho and instead choose to pack in a charcuterie board, I mention it here. Read works like the ones you want to write, but read other things as well. Read all the genres. Read hybrid works. Read experimental works. Read works in translation and in other languages. Read children's books. When you stumble upon something you love, reread it, and then reread it again. When you discover those authors who are doing things you admire, pay close attention to their sentence structure, the way they transition between ideas, the ways they move back and forth through time. Notice first sentences and last sentences, paragraph breaks and chapter breaks. Appreciate how and when and to what effect they vary their sentences. Look for phrases that recur. Notice the way tension builds in the story, the way the characters deepen and grow. Trace and retrace the narrative arcs. Read their work aloud to hear their voices. Notice how and when their characters speak. Memorize your favorite sentences so their rhythms seep into your subconscious. Then consider ways to integrate those craft elements into your own writing. This is not stealing. You are not taking their words, only the age-old techniques that they learned from someone before them and that those writers learned from writers before them and on and on through the ages. The more knowledge you have stored, the more strategies you will have at the ready when you sit down to write. In other words, fill your pack with everything you might need to make it up the mountain alive.

I also highly recommend reading books about craft, particularly books about writing memoir but also books about writing in general or books specific to other genres. In addition to the writers I've already referenced here, read Anne Lamott (*Bird by Bird*), Natalie Goldberg (*Writing Down the Bones, Wild Mind*, etc.), Bill Roorbach (*Writing Life Stories*), Mary Karr (*The Art of Memoir*), Dinty Moore (*Crafting the Personal Essay*), Elizabeth Gilbert (*Big Magic*), Annie Dillard (*The Writing Life*), or any of the other writers mentioned here or whom you discover along the way. Some online journals, such as *Brevity* and *Literary Hub*, also feature terrific essays on writing craft.

You don't need to overdo the preparation. One bottle of wine will probably do you for a quick overnight trip, and a few good writing techniques, such as perfecting the art of reflection, will go a long way. Do not treat this as a multiple-choice test. Do not cram the night before a big writing deadline. Do not overwhelm yourself. Know that you have time, a lifetime, really, to learn all that you need to know. And, most of all, do not confuse learning *how to write* with *actually writing* because, no matter how well you pack, in order to get to the summit, you still have to lace up your boots and do this the hard way—one foot in front of the other, straight up that mountain. Cheers to you! You've got this.

Now grab me half a canned peach and a tumbler full of wine and get started.

It's going to be a long night.

LOST IN THE WOODS

Writing Your Way Home

One sunny, crisp, fall day, my husband and I set out hiking on an impossible-to-get-lost-on, five-mile loop in the Pisgah National Forest near Pink Beds picnic area. The sky was Colorado blue, the forest floor blanketed with yellow. About halfway along the trail, we stopped to rest on a log near the river. We sipped water, ate a couple of protein bars, then, warmed from the walk, I took off my down vest and shed a couple of the layers beneath—an oversized gray sweatshirt, a plush purple jacket. I put the clothes in my backpack along with my phone, then slipped my vest back on.

"I'm going to take a trail break," I said as I stood.

David nodded, picked up my pack, and went to wait by the trail. It was late afternoon, the forest mainly deserted, so I was considering just peeing out in the open when a woman walked briskly down the trail. Like me, she wore a red vest, and she had short, gray hair. *We're twins,* I had time to think. And then she was gone.

Venturing farther into the woods, I found a spot, did my business, then walked back to meet David. When I got to the trail, however, he was nowhere in sight. The woods were eerily silent, the only sounds the rustling leaves and the gurgling river nearby. I began calling for him, calmly at first, then louder, more insistently. Where could he have gone? Just beyond the spot where I expected we would meet, a path veered to the left off the main trail. An orange blaze on a tree across from the path indicated the correct way, but David was colorblind and couldn't see the blazes. Could he have walked a little ahead and taken a wrong turn?

"It's a good thing you have me with you," I often joked when he walked right past a blaze marking a turn.

Now, I considered following the other route for a while just to see if David had taken a wrong turn, but what if he came back here while I was gone? I reached into my vest pocket for my phone, but just as quickly I remembered my phone was in my backpack—with David—a fact that was largely irrelevant since we likely didn't have cell service out here anyway. My next thought was that I should simply head back toward the parking lot, but I didn't have a trail map, and there were a few turns I was fuzzy on. What if I, too, got lost?

This was not a rational thought. One way or the other, the trail eventually led back to the parking lot. Still, what would I do when I got there if David wasn't there? He had the car keys, and it would take hours to walk down to the ranger station where I might find more people, and it would be dark by then. And then I worried that David was some-where worrying about me. Had I somehow misunderstood the plan? Up until now, I had been assuming that he was the one who was lost, but what if the opposite were true? What if *I* had gotten lost from *him*? It was also possible that David had gotten annoyed by how long I had taken and gone ahead. This seemed unlikely. He always waited on me. *Always*. But had I been gone longer than I realized?

None of this made any sense. I needed to talk to someone who could help me reason through this, but other than the solitary woman and a group of three hikers who had passed us earlier, I had seen no one. Now, I tried to remember if the three hikers had seemed normal, sane, not serial killer-y. They had been young, in their twenties, and they had not been dressed like hikers but more like hunters—camo jackets, blue jeans. Glassy-eyed and boisterous, they had been decidedly *unhikerlike*.

"Let's put some distance between us," I had said to David when they passed us.

At the time, I had assumed they were harmless in a let's-go-out-in-the-woods-and-get-blazed sort of way, but now, in retrospect, they seemed menacing. What if they had backtracked and found David alone? What if they had knocked him over the head and thrown him into the river where he had been attacked by one of the dozens of beavers living there? A couple of summers before, a rabid beaver had attacked a paddleboarder in an Asheville lake (Beaver Lake, to be exact!), so it wasn't completely unheard-of. It was possible—not likely, but possible—and, at the moment, it seemed about as likely as anything else. Already, I could hear myself telling the cops when I finally alerted them, "I just stepped off the trail for a minute, and when I came back, he had vanished." In any case, it was now clear to me that I had two choices—stay in place and hope that David returned or head toward the parking lot.

If I stayed in place, he would likely come back here to find me when he could—*if* he could. However, it was late afternoon, and if I lingered too long, it would be dark before I made it back to the car. Deciding that the best course of action would be to continue, I walked slowly. Every few feet, I called for David, and, finally, after I had gone about a half mile, I saw him—khaki pants, a long-sleeved gray T-shirt, green backpack. *A mirage.* He leaned against an oak tree, facing me, facing the way we had come. Clutching my stomach with one hand, I placed my other palm against my breastbone.

"*Where* have you been?" I asked when I could finally speak.

The sight of him was so unexpected, the whole situation so surreal, that I half expected him to say he had been held at gunpoint, then dropped off at this exact tree. Instead, when he spoke, his voice was a smooth stone.

"Where have *you* been?" he said. His beard twitched gently—a smile.

"I was scared," I said. A reprimand.

"I thought you were with me," he said. An explanation.

Gradually, the story unfolded. While he had waited for me on the path, he had heard someone approach. Without looking back to confirm that this person was, in fact, me, he had simply continued walking.

"That brook sure is babbling," he said to "me."

"It sure is," "I" said.

It was not until "I" asked him if he had encountered any wildlife along the trail that anything struck him as strange.

"Not any wildlife that you haven't seen," he started to say, but as he turned around to speak, he realized his mistake.

"My wife!" he screamed.

The woman said nothing in response, simply stepped aside while he hurried back down the trail the way he had come. This was his account. However, I took issue with a few of his points. For one, the word *hurried* did not seem entirely accurate.

"You were *not* hurrying," I said. "You were leaning against a tree when I found you."

"I saw you coming," he said.

As we headed together toward the parking lot, I stuck close to him.

"I have to pee again," I said, "but I'm just going to wait."

We meandered through rhododendron thickets, past thick ferns and tall pines, over bogs covered with wooden walkways.

"You didn't look at her at all?" I asked.

"No."

"You just went walking on without even checking to be sure it was me?"

"Who else is out here, Jennifer?"

Three highly suspicious millennials and a woman who looks just like me, I wanted to say. He must have at least glanced out of the corner of his eye, somehow gotten the impression of me there on the trail before he had headed on. I pressed him on this.

"Maybe," he finally said. "I could have."

"I cannot believe you could just walk off with another woman," I said.

I had made the point already, but it seemed worth underscoring. David and I had been married for close to thirty years, and most of the insecurities I had had early in our marriage—that he might one day run off with some-one more attractive and more interesting or at least some-one with better organizational skills and a more lucrative career—had faded. What frightened me more now was the idea that the things that made me *me* might one day cease to exist in the same way they once had, that as I aged, I would become generic, replaceable. Eventually, any gray-haired, red-vest-wearing lady would be a suitable substitute for me. *Close enough.*

When we finally reached our car, David wanted to discuss our dinner plans, but as we headed down the mountain, I was stuck back on the trail, at the intersection where I may not have been lost, but my husband was lost to me. *Twins,* I had thought. *Close enough.* My thoughts were sluggish, dulled from exercise and the warm air pulsing through the vents and the swaying of the car around the curves. It was dark now, not in town where there would be another thirty minutes of daylight, but here in the forest where trees formed a canopy over the road, and something about the strangeness of the night—the stillness of the forest, the vacant, black sky—took me back to another night, in 1983, soon after I first met David.

One night during my last year of high school, my friend Mary Ann and I had filled two extra-large convenience store cups with Kahlua and half-and-half and headed for the forest. We rode in Mary Ann's BMW with the windows down, the Styrofoam cups wedged between our thighs. A Virginia Slim menthol rested in Mary Ann's right hand. When she spoke, she took both hands off the wheel and turned completely to face me, her blond hair whipping her face. I held a joint between my front teeth, a Bic lighter in one hand. After several failed attempts, I finally managed to light it. I sucked in hard and held my breath. Mary Ann tossed her cigarette butt out the window, and as we passed the joint back and forth, Madonna's "Borderline" blared on the tape deck. When we got to the part about the woman in the song losing her mind, Mary Ann floored the gas and, just as the speedometer reached ninety, cut the car lights.

It was such a small memory from so very long ago, but as David and I passed the ranger station near the forest entrance, it all returned to me—the sharp scent of the weed, the desolateness of the woods, the sound of our voices rising through the darkness. What did my husband see now when he looked at me? Did he remember the bold and reckless girl I had been, the girl who later that same night retrieved his spare house key, snuck inside, and slipped naked into his bed? Or did he see only the fuzzy remnants of her—gray hair, a swath of red fabric, the safer, more tempered version of the girl he had once known?

"I'm going to have nightmares," I said to him now.

"Because you got lost in the woods?"

"Because you *left* me," I corrected him. "Because you find me replaceable. Because any similar woman will do."

He paused for just a beat before he spoke.

"That's ridiculous," he said. "That's just not true."

But I was back on that trail, stuck somewhere between where I had been and where I might go, remembering a girl who no longer existed, a woman I no longer knew.

The fact is, when you are not prepared for it, getting separated (or losing someone, depending on how you look at it) can be wildly disorienting. It can send you spinning into an uncertain future or staggering back to the fractured memories of your adolescence, and memory, like perception, can be a tricky thing. We often think of memory as objective, quantifiable. It is either correct, or it is wrong. However, the reality is much murkier than that, an essay question versus a fill-in-the-blank question. There is what you remember and what you *think* you remember. There is what you believe you saw and what you actually saw. There is what your mother told you about the trip to Maine that summer and what your sibling recalls and the family photo you have seen so many times you think you remember it, but, well, who knows, really? In fact, now you have tried to remember the trip so many times that you can smell the saltwater, see the lobster juice oozing onto the newspaper, hear the revving of the boat motor, but even in the remembering, you are changing the memory, altering it to suit the story you now believe to be absolutely, definitively true.

Radiolab produced a fabulous podcast on this topic titled "Memory and Forgetting." One of my Vermont College of Fine Arts mentors, novelist and memoirist Connie May Fowler, recommended this to me when I was just beginning my MFA program, and it changed the way I thought about memories but also about truth and fabrication (i.e., imagination) in memoir. The podcast explores the notion of imprinting, of remembering an event so many times that you actually alter the original memory. The "real memory," whatever that is, can no longer be retrieved. It has been, by virtue of your remembering it, permanently altered, a memory of a memory. How, then, given the unreliability of memory, can we create stories that are true (or, at least, as true as they ought to be)?

One way to approach this is to acknowledge that, though the details of a story may get murky over time, the emotional truth of the story remains. Your perspective of a particular event (i.e., the way you understand a story) may shift as you move away from the events, but the way you originally experienced that event, the real, visceral recollections you carry in

your body, do not change. Though Robert Olen Butler is a
fiction writer, his series of lectures compiled by Janet Burro-
way in the craft book *From Where You Dream* nonetheless offers
memoir writers a useful perspective on how to use those recollections to build vivid, compelling scenes rich in sensory
detail. Butler believes that writers must delve deeply into
their creative minds and enter a meditative state he describes
as "dreamstorming." This deep daydreaming allows writers
to experience (or reexperience) the story in their imagina-
tions as they translate it to the page.

In other words, what do you see, hear, taste, smell, feel?
Get it all down as soon as you can after an event you want
to write about, while it is as close to a "real" or "true"
memory as possible. Do not edit or revise at this point.
Just write and write and write. The more time you spend
recalling and writing, the more details you will remember.
Perhaps you will recall not only the oozing lobster juice but
also the server who handed you a stack of napkins and said,
"Here's a crap-ton of napkins." You will recall the stream
that ran by the picnic table where you ate outside, the fisherman at the table next to you, his red face and deep laugh,
the way he tucked his napkin into his shirt and the way
it was splotched with butter, and the way the sun turned
the mountains purple as you drove back to the motel, all
stuffed and sunburned, your arms aching from sea kayaking
all day.

One of the best examples of original, gobsmacking sensory details I know can be found in Annie Dillard's 1982
story "Total Eclipse." In this piece from *Teaching a Stone to
Talk*, Dillard offers a master class in how to use sensory detail
to create mood and tone and meaning. Consider this passage

in which Dillard describes the eerie otherworldliness of the eclipse:

> The sky was navy blue. My hands were silver. All the distant hills' grasses were finespun metal which the wind laid down. I was watching a faded color print of a movie filmed in the Middle Ages; I was standing in it, by some mistake. I was standing in a movie of hillside grasses filmed in the Middle Ages. I missed my own century, the people I knew, and the real light of day.

Dillard goes on to describe the disorienting effects of the eclipse, the feeling of being removed entirely from time and place. The sight of her husband, Gary, is "familiar and wrong," and the skin on his face moves "like thin bronze plating that would peel." Nothing has prepared Dillard for this devastating moment. "What I seemed to be standing in, was all the wrecked light that the memories of the dead could shed upon the living world," she says. When Dillard tells this story, readers don't so much see or understand the eclipse as *feel* it, feel the "dark shadow speeding at us . . . like thunder." Through her vivid, compelling imagery, Dillard leaves us terrified in the same way that Joyce Carol Oates does in "Where Are You Going? Where Have You Been?" or Flannery O'Connor does in "A Good Man Is Hard to Find." The details and descriptions are not only captivating; they are inseparable from the truth of the story.

When I introduce creative nonfiction to new students, I often draw a Venn diagram on the board and put fiction on one side and nonfiction on the other. We talk about what makes each genre distinct. Then we discuss what to put in the center. Where do these genres overlap? The students note things like plot, character development, interiority, scene setting, and narrative arc, so we add them to the center. Both genres employ all these things. But one thing beginning creative nonfiction writers often fail to see is where we borrow—or could borrow or, even, *ought* to borrow—from poetry. Poets know how to create emotional intensity and the value of laboring over diction and syntax, by chiseling away at words, by molding and shaping images and sounds to unveil stark, emotional truths. In "Total Eclipse," Dillard does it all—plot, setting, character development, lyrical language, exquisitely rendered scenes.

When I was younger, I wanted to be a poet, and many days I still fantasize about having that sort of mind, that sort of soul. The truth is, though, I am too imprecise, my thoughts too disjointed and wandering, to ever be a real poet. I need the structure of prose to keep me in line. Still, I am grateful for the genre fluidness that has permeated recent literature. Poems are still poems, but they are no longer *only* poems. Thanks to writers like Maggie Nelson (*Bluets*), Carmen Maria Machado (*In the Dream House*), Sarah Manguso (*300 Arguments*), and Claudia Rankine (*Citizen*), poems have given rise to lyric essays and vignettes and prosetry and prose poems. The possibilities are endless, and experimentation with form—veering off the marked trails, so to speak— can open up new ways of seeing and remembering and understanding.

Memory, like truth, is complicated. I am the girl riding shotgun and belting out "Borderline" through the dark forest and the woman my husband sees out of the corner of his eye on an impossible-to-get-lost-on trail and the peeing-behind-the-bushes woman who will soon return to the trail and find her husband missing. In order to capture such complex truths, memoir writers must rely on sensory details to reveal the narrator's longing (or, to put it another way, the way it is so often put in writing classes, to illuminate what is at stake for the narrator).

Case in point: One day last June, a few months into the pandemic, I ventured down to the blueberry bushes on our property to pick some berries. It was a simple task, one I had done many times before, but for some reason the moment seemed monumental, and in writing about it later, I struggled mightily to capture the quiet, intense aching I felt. The piece I was writing was brief, the situation not inherently difficult to write about, yet so much seemed to be at stake. So much *was* at stake. I just had not yet figured out what that was, so I wrote and rewrote and rewrote again, and finally I realized why it was so hard. Just as when I had been writing about the snake that fell from our roof and onto my daughter's lap, I was trying to capture what was *not* on the page, the feeling between the words. I revised again and again and again until I came up with the following:

> Despite the early hour, the air was already humid, and days of rain had left the bank slippery with rotting weeds and leaves. Still, it was the perfect time for berry picking, just after the fruit turned deep purply-blue and before the crows cleaned out the vines. As I paused at the top of the hill, gnats swarmed my face, and a line of sweat trickled down my bra. Wearing jeans, a T-shirt under a long-sleeved flannel shirt buttoned tightly at the throat and wrists, knee socks, knee-high muck boots, a neck buff and a wide-brimmed hat,

I was decidedly overdressed, but berry picking here was not for the faint of heart.

Since my husband and I had moved to this wooded hollow almost seven years before, the dozen or so bushes had grown gangly and unruly, full of awkward, spindly limbs and infested with all stripes of flying, biting creatures. The bushes were not wild, but they weren't exactly tame either. Planted decades earlier, they were aligned in front of a handful of blackberry bushes and near the foundation of an old barn, and though I had never pruned them or weeded them or given them a dose of whatever you gave blueberry bushes to encourage growth, I had come to think of them as mine, as my compensation for living in a century-old cabin with a leaky roof and more than its share of venomous snakes and fist-sized spiders. In the world outside of this wooded bubble that had slowly begun to feel like mine, all manner of chaos reigned, but out here, a mile away from the mailbox, two miles from the main road, the world fell away from me or I from it. I was Violet Beauregarde in Willy Wonka's chocolate factory, Laura and Lizzie in Rossetti's "Goblin Market," Maggie Nelson in *Bluets*—consumed with blue.

Working my way into the thicket, I checked the ground for roots, branches, and, especially, the tell-tale signs of copperheads: thick, hourglass-patterned bodies, flat, triangular heads. I hadn't ever seen a copperhead in this exact spot, but we had seen many around our house, and it was enough to know that they could be here, that the conditions were right. I picked carefully, moving in concentric circles, parting branches and dropping ripe fruit into the metal mixing bowl I carried in one hand. High in the pines, a murder of crows complained, my presence an intrusion on their breakfast buffet. In the field below, hens scratched in the dirt, and ten goats, two bucks in one, three does and their offspring in the other, wandered from the two adjacent barns to wait under the overhang for the dewy grass to dry.

The bucks were past their prime, their seasons of ravenous mating behind them, but they nonetheless bellowed robustly across the pasture to their one-time lovers—two caprine catcallers. Once, my body, too, had burned with a fierce, spiky heat. Once, when I was young, I had leapt from a second-story ledge to meet my lover by the side of a moonlit road where he sat, car idling, windows rolled down, Lynyrd Skynyrd blaring from the tape deck. Once, I did lines on a floor-length mirror with a wannabe hippie I almost loved. Once, I absconded to the Midwest to live in a boxcar next to an abandoned house where wild foxes roamed. Once, I swam in a thermal pool by an island in the middle of the Atlantic Ocean, smeared butter over a cob of volcano-cooked corn, caressed hot, black sand with my bare toes. Next to a lake in Waterton, Canada, I petted a wild deer. I ate butter-drenched, garlicky eels in Barcelona, drank thick, dark chocolate at Angelina's in Paris, soared on a zipline over an Appalachian forest.

These may not seem like daring things, yet, for me, they had been, or at least I had once believed them to be. Now, my life had become a series of tamped-down cravings, my indulgences whittled down to a manageable few—punk-purple hair dye, a second glass of Chardonnay, an afternoon spent binge-watching *Schitt's Creek*. And what did I expect at my age anyway? When I was in fourth grade, I had a teacher who corrected her students for using the word *starving* on the grounds that the word was overkill, too big a word for a gentle gnawing in the guts that signaled it was time for lunch or a snack, too flippant in light of all those people around the world who were actually starving. After all, what did a bunch of nine-year-olds know about hunger, about desire of any kind, really? And what did I know of it now, all these years later, after a lifetime spent yearning for something always just beyond my reach? Still, just when I thought it might be gone for good, here in the berry patch, I hungered for a new sensation, something to pierce through the ordinariness of my life and remind me that I was still among the living.

But, of course, there was always a price to pay, and here in the blueberry thicket, the cost for an extravaganza of blueberry delights was steep: a good, strong dose of chiggers. Chiggers were the stealthy, vile, microscopic, spider-like creatures that infested this thicket. When you were least expecting it, they burrowed in the warmest parts of your body—under your arms, behind your knees, under your breasts, between your legs. The larvae bore holes in your skin, then feasted on the cells inside. According to an old wives' tale, a thin layer of clear nail polish applied to the welts would smother the mites inside, but, actually, by the time you noticed the itching, the bugs had actually already fallen off, their feeding frenzy over, the satiated larvae well on their way to maturity. You could mitigate the damage, batten the hatches, brace for the long, sleepless night ahead, but once the chiggers had had a go at you, there wasn't much you could do.

Still. I wanted what I wanted: jam, pancakes, syrup, smoothies, cobblers, cakes, muffins, compotes, tarts. And so I pushed aside thoughts of the ethereal, shadowy images that had appeared on my screen earlier when I had googled "chiggers" and instead focused on the gurgling of the creek in the distance, on the gentle crooning of mother goats. By the time the sun rose over the pasture, and the goats had ventured into the tall grass, I had stripped the lower branches of berries, but clusters hung high in one of the bushes, just beyond my grasp. I tried reaching the fruit from different angles—from the side, from underneath, from the steepest part of the bank—to no avail. Finally, I jumped, grabbed the limb, pulled it down, and pinned it beneath one arm. Spiders and inchworms poured onto my shirt. I shook them off and wedged the limb deeper into my armpit so that one hand was free to pick the berries that now dangled chest-high in front of me.

Later that night, when I woke frantically clawing the welts between my legs and on the nipple of my right breast, I would wonder if this was the moment when the chiggers had scuttled down the neck of my shirt and into my bra, into the soft pits of my underarms, the warm waistband of my jeans. The itching would not be pain, exactly, more a cousin of pain—fierce and nauseating—and I would vow once again to be more careful next time, more prudent. But in the midst of the berry patch, I was emboldened, careless, maybe even carefree ("Be childlike, not childish," my hippie lover once told me), and I picked and picked and picked until my fingers were blue, my hair damp and frizzy, until visions of blueberry pancakes drenched in blueberry syrup oozed over me, leaving only the hot, thick stillness of this place.

Perhaps I still did not adequately capture the loss and longing of that moment. Perhaps I could not. But in the end, I was satisfied that somewhere in the space between those words, I had captured something of the beauty and pain of being both of this world and not, of knowing that my time here is temporary, that I will not always be. How do we write about abstract ideas like pain and loss and desire and regret? Like the poets, we ground the abstract in the concrete, in real, everyday images and experiences, in scenes that zoom in on a particular place and time and tell the reader, "Hey, stop here. Here is where I want you to pay particular attention." What is it you want to convey? And what sensory details will best lead you to that moment? Get down all the details you can recall as you are writing, and then, once the story begins to take shape and form and meaning, you can go back and chisel away, selecting those details that create the right mood and tone for your piece, which, by the very way they sound on the page and the images they evoke, transform your story into something universal, a truth your reader may then claim as her own as well.

BUSHWHACKING

Digging for Truer Truths

When I am hiking in DuPont, backpackless, mapless hikers often stop to ask me for directions: *Is this the way to the water- fall? Is the lake over there? Does this road lead to the trail?* Each time, I struggle to contain my frustration. DuPont covers more than ten thousand acres, including almost ninety miles of trails, six major waterfalls, and five lakes, so if you want to go to a particular place, you are going to need a map.

On the other hand, if you are willing to wander around a bit, to get turned around a bit, to try this trail because it is cool and shady and that trail because it meanders past a broad field and that one because it runs alongside a wide creek, then you may not find the one waterfall the guide- book told you was a "must-see." Perhaps, though, you will stumble upon the patch of pink and yellow lady slippers that sprawl along a certain trail each May, the bear that fre- quents the blackberry bushes near Thomas Cemetery each summer, the deer that thrive along Reasonover Creek trail, or the turkeys that meander along the hill along Airstrip Trail each fall. What I am saying is that when you go into the woods without a map, you must be comfortable getting lost. You must learn to embrace the journey, which is not as easy as it sounds. At least not for me.

My friend Susan loves to take her five dogs bushwhacking through the Pisgah National Forest. She starts at a trailhead on the parkway, say the one to Beaverdam Gap, then heads across the street to an unmarked trail and follows it all the way down to where Laurel Creek meets Mills River. And then she suddenly wonders if the trail up ahead will take her back to the parkway a different way and off she will go, with five or six dogs running ahead of or behind her. If, after a suitable period of time, the trail has not emerged where she expects it to, she simply wanders through the woods until she comes upon another trail that she recognizes. For Susan, getting lost is not *beside* the point. It *is* the point. Though I would prefer that she take her cell phone and an energy bar or, at the very least, a water bottle *just in case*, I get it. I get that she loves the freedom she feels in the woods, the challenge of finding her way out, the delight she takes in everything she discovers along the way.

"The dogs and I found the best swimming hole today," she will say. Or "I found the best blackberry patch." Or "I saw the cutest (insert ferocious wild animal here)."

In addition to being an avid runner and hiker, Susan is also a musician and a writer. She sings and plays the guitar. She writes nonfiction, fiction, and poetry. She is also a gifted high school English teacher. We met when my daughter was in her class, and we got to be friends a few years later when we took a writing class together. Later, we taught together for one wild year, and her example, as a writer and teacher and adventurer, is one that I carry with me. I wish I were able to bring the same energy to the classroom that Susan does, the same enthusiasm she exudes when she is meandering through the woods or writing an essay or playing her guitar or singing.

Susan's passion for discovery is inextricably linked to her creativity. Curiosity is what makes a writer a writer, a hiker a hiker, a teacher a teacher. Getting turned around is how you discover what you're made of, and her joy in these moments is visceral. It works its way into everything she does. She ambles along through the woods until she finds something interesting, and then she celebrates her discovery: *How about that? A swimming hole, a berry patch, a bear all in one day!* Her amazement is contagious. It bolsters me. Normally a cautious stick-in-the-mud, around Susan, I want to be the sort of person who accidentally bumps into a berry patch versus the sort of person who googles "berry patches, Blue Ridge Parkway" and then asks Siri for help finding my destination. I want to be more adventurous, more willing to traverse off the beaten path, to, in Thoreau's words, "march to the beat of a different drummer."

Getting good at getting lost takes practice, though, lots and lots of practice, and I am still working on it. I tend to panic too soon, to think of all the ways things could go badly wrong before I get to the good parts. Sometimes, I am right. Bad things do happen—or almost happen. Once, Susan and I were hiking on a trail off the parkway with my daughter and another woman. Because of Covid, we were all out of work or working remotely on our own schedules, so we had all day to wander around the woods. We had seven dogs with us, including Susan's six-month-old Jack Russell puppy, Rudy. All the dogs were off leash except for one. Coming around a bend, as Susan and I were laughing about how we had gotten lost at this intersection of the Flat Creek Trail the last time we were here, my daughter touched my arm.

"Do you hear that?" she asked.

I hadn't. But then I did—a swarm of cicadas or bees or . . . All at once, the dogs were snarling and yapping at something just off the trail. Then, above the thick under-brush, a long, thick, angry rattlesnake appeared, its tail shaking like a tambourine, its body weaving through the air. *Dancing*, we would say later. *Writhing. Like Kaa from* The Jungle Book. Frantic, we screamed for the dogs, who, alarmed by our alarm, all raced back to us. We gathered everyone on leashes and eventually arrived back to our car, four women and seven dogs, all safe and sound.

However, that night, every time I drifted to sleep, I jerked awake, the image of that writhing snake just inches from the dogs, just feet from us, still fresh in my mind. Rudy was tiny and unlikely to survive a deadly bite. What if Alex hadn't heard it just when she did? What if the dogs hadn't listened when we called them back? What if Rudy had gotten bitten, and we hadn't been able to get him up the mountain and to the vet in time? *What if, what if, what if . . .*

Both in writing and in life, I tend to get overwhelmed by possibilities. What if my writing isn't interesting to anyone but me? What if I sound ridiculous? What if I am too old to be doing this? What if no one ever reads it? What if I never publish anything again? *What if, what if, what if . . .* The fear can be incapacitating, like when you are out hiking and you encounter what you at first glance believe to be a snake, but as you get closer, you see that the snake is, in fact, a stick. No matter. Once you have seen a snake, it is difficult, almost impossible, to *unsee* the snake. And even if you could unsee it, you would have seen a snake morph into a stick, and what confidence could you possibly have that that same stick would not morph right back into a snake again? You are bigger than the snake, of course. And perhaps it isn't even a venomous snake. Perhaps it is a harmless black snake or a little ringneck. Still, you are afraid to move, afraid to go forward or back. Because you remember the time you went down the wrong path and you found a rattlesnake (or it found you), you want so badly to get it right the first time.

Similarly, every writer who has ever tried to say anything knows the deep fear that often stands in our way of getting words on the page. Perhaps you once wrote something that you later deemed to be trash or that someone else said was trash or that you submitted nine hundred times and it got rejected nine hundred times so now you firmly believe it to be trash. For a period of time, you are frozen, literarily speaking. After an experience like that, it can be hard to toss the cat out of your chair and flick the tortilla chip crumbs and PB2 powder off your keyboard and start writing again. Chances are, though, you will encounter many such moments in your writing life, and the thing that will separate you from the person who simply throws up her hands or throws in the towel or whatever throwing metaphor you want to use is that you will have practiced tenacity and fortitude and resilience on the trail. You will have what it takes to face a menacing obstacle and move past it.

When I was in my twenties with three young children, I went back to graduate school to get a master's degree in English, and for my first creative writing workshop, I wrote a piece about my relationship with my ex-husband, about how violent and abusive and just generally terrifying he had been throughout our marriage and throughout the time I was pregnant with our daughter. The piece I wrote for workshop that day was my first attempt to write about these events, which were still very fresh at the time. When I finished reading my story to our group, my instructor was silent while my classmates talked about style and tone and so on. And then he said, and though I remember this as being very dramatic, with loud throat-clearing and a dramatic pause—that may be hyperbole—but still, more than twenty years later, I remember his words exactly: "It sounds like the narrator in this story is just as crazy as her husband."

In retrospect, it occurs to me that this teacher may simply have been, in his own way, urging me to see what was on the page and to revise accordingly, but at the time, with the abuse so fresh in my mind and spirit, it felt like a scathing criticism of me personally. I had encountered a rattlesnake in the trail. Or a stick that looked like a rattlesnake. How was I to know the difference? And, in any case, how was I to move forward knowing that everyone in my class now believed I was crazy?

The answer was that I had to keep writing, keep reading, keep studying craft, keep sharing my work, keep writing and rewriting until I got it right. Though the words on the page did not yet fully reflect my experience, one day they would. I would revise and revise and revise until the story became more true, until I was able to reveal more of the emotional truth of my experience. By incorporating more reflective voice (a technique Sue William Silverman explores in depth in her wonderful memoir craft book *Fearless Confessions*), I was able to explain why I kept going back to a man who held a razor blade to my throat and choked me unconscious. I was able to explain how I kept believing he would change, that I could change him. I was able to describe how everything I had experienced up until that moment in my life had led me to believe in happy endings and to explore how that vision of the happy ending had, for a time, rendered me helpless. I was able to show how I eventually realized that the responsibility for creating a happy ending now rested solely on me. I was able to say that, even though it was the hardest thing I had ever done, I had gotten my baby to safety. I had rescued us both. The events, you see, had not changed, but the story on the page changed as I came to better understand how I ended up with such a man and the courage it took to finally leave him. Through the use of reflective voice, I was able to convey to the reader this new, deeper understanding of what had occurred.

Learning how and when to use reflective voice was perhaps the most challenging and rewarding part of my MFA program. Before then, my work was full of decent scenes. I could do setting. I could do dialogue. I knew how to engage the senses. But what I didn't know was how to make sense of any of it for me or for the reader, which, it turns out, is key to memoir writing. Readers know what to make of a story because you, the writer, frame the story in such a way that they understand it in a certain way. You are the lens through which they see your story. This means, of course, that you must first understand the story yourself, which is easier than it sounds. Sometimes, I start to write thinking a story is about one thing, and then it suddenly morphs into something completely different. When this happens, I have learned to pay attention to where the story wants to go, to consider how to contextualize the experience for myself first, and, later, for my readers.

Another case in point: Years ago, I wrote a story about traveling out west when I was a kid. My mother, father, brother, and I drove all the way from our home in North Carolina to the Grand Canyon, and somewhere along the way, I left a beloved set of stuffed dogs at a motel. I was so distraught that my parents had the dogs rush-shipped to the next hotel where we were staying. When I first wrote the story, I thought it was a funny tale about my anxious, histrionic behavior. Then, because I talked about a pathological fear of an imminent Second Coming, I thought it was about belief and faith and doubt. Still later, I began to see that it was a complicated story about family dynamics. Each time I sat down to write, something new emerged, and each time I had to reconsider what the story was about and, therefore, where it was going. With each telling, it became a richer, fuller version of the story—*more true*, if you will. In fact, whenever I am drawn to tell a story, but I can't figure out what exactly it is about, I write myself a note in large, bold ink: WHAT IS THIS ABOUT? Somehow, I find it reassuring. Even asking the question lets me know that I am writing my way into truer truths.

Writing your way into this deeper knowing means having faith in the meandering, evolving nature of truth, in the process of writing past the fear of metaphorical snakes into a more fully realized version of your truth. Writing then becomes not just something you do. It becomes who you are. Therefore, like Susan out bushwhacking in the woods, you do not need to panic when you have lost your bearings. You can get lost and find your way back. Your first draft might be nonsensical, but you must keep going, channel your inner Susan until you stumble upon something breathtaking. Perhaps, for example, you will come upon a blackberry thicket, and you will be so busy admiring the thick berries that you almost don't see the black bear sitting just a few feet away. And when you write about him later, he will be sitting on his haunches, pulling fat fruit from the vine, looking for all the world like a contented old man smoking a pipe. He will remind you of why you went into the woods in the first place, and you will be amazed.

And we will all be amazed right along with you.

FINDING YOUR STRIDE

Toning Your Writing Muscles

In the past couple of years, I have taken up running again, which is not to say that I exactly stopped for any extended period, but over the years, I have had lulls and upticks, and I am currently experiencing an uptick. Still, as much as I love running and as grateful as I am to have a job with flexible hours and to live where I have easy access to miles of gorgeous running trails, I still have days when I have difficulty getting started. I am too cold or too hot. I am too tired and too sore from my last workout. I am too hungry or I've eaten too much. I have too much work to do. I am bored with my route. I find the mere thought of all the preparation daunting—finding a clean running bra and my favorite pair of Bombas, choosing which dog I am going to take and breaking it gently to the ones I am not taking because they are too old and infirm or young and unpredictable. I have to find my backpack, my water bottle, my protein bar, the dog's leader, harness, and leash. During the pandemic, when going outside to hike or run has been my only activity for days at a time, my list of essential materials has been expanded to include hand sanitizer, a Buff, two masks.

"It's like having a newborn again," I complain to my daughter, who is also my running partner. "Every time I leave the house, I have to pack diapers and lotion and the wipes and pacifiers and toys and teething rings and bottles . . ."

My tone is whiny—put upon and put out. However, since Alex moved back home to ride out the pandemic, we have taken turns being the adult in the relationship.

"Okay," she says. "Okay, that's enough. Let's just go."

Even with a running buddy, going out into the woods is a production, and sometimes I am exhausted before I ever get started. On those days, I have to drag myself out the front door, but I do it. I may not always run. Some days, I do a fast walk instead. Some days, I do a slow walk, but I miss getting outside only a few days a year, usually when I am sick or traveling. I push myself to go because I know I will feel better when I do. I will be in a better mood. I will have more energy, more clarity. I will remember things I had previously forgotten. I will feel calmer, steadier, less pissed off at the world. I will no longer come unhinged at maskless people and people with out-of-control dogs and bikers who refuse to yield to hikers. I will be zen and unruffled, the very picture of expansiveness and generosity. At least for a couple of hours.

Knowing this makes starting my run easier. But what really gets me through on those days is simply the fact that my body and mind don't always operate in sync. My mind may be back home curled up in my recliner with a good mystery, but the second I hit the trail and turn on my music, my body remembers what to do. Off I go, over the rooty, muddy stretch, across the first bridge and then the highway before turning right and heading up the trail to the North Slope. Sometimes, I am halfway through before I am even fully conscious of the exertion. My mind is resistant, but my body has been doing this for so long, it does it on its own until my mind catches up. (I once had a Presbyterian minister explain religion this way to me: as an unbeliever, I could still attend church because everyone else would believe for me until I began to believe myself. Unfortunately, church did not work out this way for me, but, fortunately, running has.)

The fact that I usually run in one of three places helps me get in a running mind-set. I smell the campfire smoke or see the fishermen waist-high in the river, and something clicks. I also always listen to the same playlist. At different times in my life, however, for various reasons, I have fixated on different songs from the list. The summer my friend April was dying from ovarian cancer, I listened to Steve Earle's "Copperhead Road" over and over. Every time it neared the end, I hit rewind. Some days, it was the only song I played for the hour I was out on the trail. I ran with my puppy, Roo, and together we leapt across puddles, scaled downed trees. We ran until we were breathless, our feet covered in mud, our tongues hanging out. We ran until my legs were numb and rocks filled my shoes and hot sweat pooled in my bra. Under the circumstances, "Copperhead Road" seemed an odd choice for a running anthem, but I was despondent and angry, and something about the narrator's sorrowful rebellion, about the wildness in Steve's voice, brought me back to myself. Fuck the establishment. Fuck law and order. Fuck God. Fuck anyone who had ever told me that good people are rewarded. There was no rhyme or reason, no purpose, no plan, no moral, no lesson. There was only the rushing river and the rippling wind and burnt whiskey and mamas crying and choppers whirling and one lone man railing at the senselessness of it all. For twenty-three hours a day, I was nearly incapacitated with grief, but for one hour a day, I ran and ran and ran until Steve Earle cleansed us both.

Later, after April's death, "Brown-Eyed Women" by the Grateful Dead was my go-to running song. Then, after that, I replayed "All You Fascists Bound to Lose," a remake of the Woody Guthrie tune by Resistance Revival Chorus and Rhiannon Giddens. Then I switched to "Cotton Fields" by Credence Clearwater Revival. At each moment in my life, these songs gave voice to something I could not yet say—a desire to recapture joy, perhaps, a longing for a particular time and place, for though I was home in the literal sense of the word, after Trump and after Covid, the world around me had morphed into something I did not recognize and did not know how to navigate. Alone in the woods, I sought to calm myself, to regroup and refuel, and the only reason I showed up again and again was, well, habit. I ran because I had run the day before and the day before that and the day before that, because I believed that if I kept showing up each day, eventually it would get easier—the run, April's death, the insanity of the Trump era, everything.

No matter how I begin a run or walk, I end feeling better than when I began, and when I miss a day out in the woods, my mind and body feel it. I am cranky, lethargic, sullen. If I miss two days, I cry at the smallest things. I can't focus on my work. I cannot hear what you are trying to tell me. If I miss more than two . . . well, you wouldn't want to stick around to find out how ill-humored I become. The woods feed me in some essential way, and I need my time there as much as I need my writing time. The exercise calms me, yes, but my senses are also fine-tuned to the natural world. Everything comes into sharper focus. Everything makes more sense. Both in writing and on the trail, I show up and do the hard work because I believe there is a big picture even when I can't see it all. And so I immerse myself in the practice and trust that showing up, even on my worst days, matters.

The key to this, I have learned, is not overthinking things, not when I am running or when I am writing. This is especially useful for me when I am stuck on a story or when I feel like I have nothing new to say or even when I am struggling with revisions. I like to make deals with myself, and sometimes I tell myself that I can spend the whole day outside if I come back and write one page about something I observed. It can be anything—a biker with spiked, bleached hair like Guy Fieri, a baby possum that chased me down a trail (who knew they did this?), a wild pig that sprinted after my mountain bike—but my rule on these days when writing is especially challenging is that I never write more than a page. In moments when I feel overwhelmed or even underwhelmed—when I am not properly *whelmed*—I remind myself to stay balanced, to take the time to rest and observe, to tuck away little nuggets of beauty that I may or may not return to later. Perhaps they will grow into something more, but even if they don't, they remind me that there is power in the here and now, and if I can capture this precise moment on the page, even briefly and imperfectly, even if no one else ever reads it, I will have done something worthwhile.

This, too, is a lesson I have learned in the woods. Reasonover Creek Trail in DuPont is a 5.2-mile trail with a dicey creek crossing near the trailhead. In summer months, the creek is often too deep to cross, even on a bike, and the partially submerged rocks strewn across the wide creek bed are often slippery. In winter, the rocks can be icy. Crossing any time of year in any fashion can be a challenge for me (though, by far, the most challenging has been crossing with a mountain bike hoisted over one shoulder). The trick, I have discovered, is to just hop on a rock and get going, to let your body move without the constraints of an overanxious mind.

If I try to reason through the best route—which rocks look steady, which one too slick, etc.—I will fall, which is really no big deal since the river is not that deep, and the only consequence will be that I will have to finish the trail with soaking wet shoes. However, for some reason, I often start out okay, one foot firmly on an exposed rock, and then I step onto the next and then the next and then, suddenly, I can't figure out how to navigate to the next one, and my legs start to tremble, and I cannot go backward or forward, and I am stuck there, consumed with the thought of falling in and getting wet and failing, failing, failing, and then my legs are rendered completely useless, and some generous soul—a hiking or biking buddy, a random stranger passing by—has to stop and trek across the rocks and offer me a hand and help me over. Barring that, I have to take the plunge and step into the knee-deep water and wade to shore, an utter and abject failure. Overthinking ruins my confidence.

This, you see, is where each writer must go, into the woods and over the difficult crossings. As writers, we cannot wait for inspiration to hit us over the head. We must develop a practice that allows our muscle memory to carry us through, and we must write freely, without overthinking it, without considering who might be offended by what we say or what we might be getting wrong and, dare I say, without too much concern about what will sell and what will not sell. There will be time to worry about these things in the revision process (and, for most of us, in the long months and perhaps years before our writing sees the light of day). But, just as when you are navigating a tricky creek crossing, when you are just setting out on your writing journey, you have to get out of your own way.

Robert Olen Butler, it seems, would agree: "There's a part of your mind you've been rewarded for all through school, and that is your literal memory," he says. "You remember things; you can talk these things back and remember details. You know literature. You've always found your self-worth there, and what I'm telling you is that literal memory is your enemy." What Butler is talking about here is the importance of creating what John Gardner called the "vivid and continuous dream." To do this, you must train your brain to step aside so that you do not meander into overanalyzing, into the dreaded "telling" versus "showing." There is a place for telling, of course. There are moments when telling is important, even necessary. However, this does not exempt the memoirist from the task of creating a believable world. (It may be real. But is it *believable?* Can the reader feel it?) One way writers create such a world is by developing fully realized scenes that immerse the reader in the writer's experiences. Another is by developing a unique narrative voice, one that readers trust to carry them over the creek crossings and through the crux of a story.

Much has been written about voice, about what it is and how one finds one's "true" voice. However, after many years of teaching, I still struggle to define this element of craft for my students and for myself. I do recognize it when I hear it, though. *Ah, that. Now, that is a strong voice,* I will say when a piece of writing hits me just right. Butler says that every piece he has ever read that falls short is lacking one essential element: yearning. I would add to this that every story I have ever not loved has lacked a strong voice. If I cannot distinguish it from all the other voices I hear, it is not yet fully realized on the page. (In my view, one of the masters of voice is Jo Ann Beard, and if you have not yet read *Boys of My Youth*, stop right here, go get it, and do not come back until you are finished reading.)

Of course, strong voices come in many forms, and for me, some of the clearest voices I hear in my head both while I am on the trail and while I am writing are those from the songs I love best. In the spring of 2021, as we ushered in the one-year anniversary of the pandemic, my running song of choice was Justin Townes Earle's "Harlem River Blues." Like most of us, Townes Earle, the son of Steve Earle (and namesake of Townes Van Zandt), led a life marked by both beauty and struggle, and at the age of thirty-eight, Townes Earle died of a drug overdose. There is this powerful line in "Harlem River Blues" that says, "I know the difference between tempting and choosing my fate." As I ran, I played the song over and over and over, and as I wrote and donned my mask to go to the grocery store and taught Zoom classes and tried to encourage my students who did not yet believe that their lives would one day be full and fun again, I was haunted by his words. Did he tempt fate one time too many? Or did he simply give up on living? The tone of the song is upbeat, a deceptively simple vessel for carrying such big questions, yet there they are.

In my young life, I often tempted fate. Now, I tend to take the safer paths, to stray from dramatic crossroads where I make decisions, which, I suppose, is a decision all its own, a decision to hold tight, lay low, burrow into the moment at hand. After all, we cannot know what tomorrow holds. We cannot approach the trail or the creek crossing or the blank page with any degree of certainty. And yet we can show up, don our running shoes and our headphones, and maybe grab a firm walking stick to aid in any precarious creek crossings because there is no shame in that. We can show up today and again tomorrow and again the next day. We can keep moving, keep jumping from stone to stone, keep plugging away, pouring strange, awkward words out into the world with the hope that one day they might get away from us, drift up a wooded hillside or skim the surface of an icy mountain river and, if we are very, very lucky, flow back to us, a song.

RUNNING UPHILL

Surviving the Tough Climbs

It was thirtysomething degrees, dark, and pouring rain when I pulled into the Guion Farm parking lot for the DuPont 5K Halloween Run. Wearing thick running tights, my grandmother's Cuddl Duds top, a long-sleeved shirt, gloves, a knit hat, and a raincoat, I made my way through dense fog to the picnic area to retrieve my race bib. Then I waited under the picnic shelter with the local middle school cross-country team for the race to begin. Hundreds of runners had registered for the event, but attendance overall was sparse, which might have had something to do with the fact that it was nine p.m., and torrential rain had been falling all day. Storm warnings, freeze warnings, and high wind warnings had been issued. Downed limbs littered the roads, and both the Davidson and French Broad Rivers were expected to soon jump their banks.

This probably should have concerned me, led me to consider that this was not the wisest thing for a painfully nearsighted, fiftysomething-year-old, sometimes jogger to do. In fact, my husband had said as much to me before I left the house. He was genuinely concerned I was going to injure myself, and, honestly, if the event had been canceled, I would gladly have stayed home with a book and a cup of hot tea. But this was Transylvania County, and it was Halloween, and, by God, the race would go on. Besides, I had been training for weeks, and I had always wanted to run in the woods at night. I had just been too chicken to do it on my own. Here in the dark, wet, foggy forest, within shouting range of a bunch of other runners, was my chance to *feel* brave. The weather would just make it more exciting, I told myself. As long as I didn't slide down and break a hip or shatter a knee, it was going to be a blast.

The route began on Buck Forest Road. When the starting time approached, I lined up with the other runners. Some were wearing costumes, but the attempts were mostly half-hearted—a few vampire fangs here and there, a wig or two. I fumbled to get my headphones in place under my knit hat. Then I pulled my raincoat hood over that, found my playlist on my phone and tucked it into a waterproof pocket, then switched on my headlamp. Later, I would realize that I had only turned on one of the two bulbs, but there, with all the other runners' lamps, it seemed adequate. The horn sounded, and we were off. At first, we stayed together, roughly a hundred diehard souls running down a gravel road in the darkness. Then, gradually, we began to spread out. Some runners tried to dodge the first puddles, but as the puddles grew into miniature ponds, most eventually gave up and just ran through them. These were the sort of people who showed up on a night like this—fatalists, the go-hard-or-go-home crowd.

After about a mile and a half, we took a left on Thomas Cemetery Trail, and soon after that, I was alone. Sloshing through puddles halfway up my calves and skidding over rocks and roots, I passed an old family burial ground and a hitching post, then crossed over a bridge. I had been on this trail many times but never at night, and this stretch was especially dark. In addition, fog and torrential rain obscured my view of anything more than a few feet in front of me, and it occurred to me that there could be all sorts of wild creatures close by—bears and bobcats and coyotes. And then I thought of Cheryl Strayed, of how, even in the face of obliterating grief, she had been brave enough to hike the Pacific Crest Trail alone. If she could hike alone in the snow-covered Rockies, I could make it around a 3.2-mile loop in the forest at night. Running is, after all, largely a mental game. If you think you can do it, you can do it.

When I was a kid, the school day I had dreaded most, next to Field Day, was the day of the Presidential Physical Fitness Test. No matter how much I practiced, I could never hold the flexed arm hang for more than two seconds, nor could I do more than one sit-up. To this day, I have nightmares about being stretched on the gym floor, my knees bent, my hands in a death grip behind my head as I strain to lift higher than just a couple of inches off the blue and red mat. I remember the sickly, rubbery smell, the teacher's tight ponytail, her strained face, her sun-spotted hands gripping the clipboard, the silence in the room while the other children in line watched and waited, terrified, I was sure, that their fate would be as bad as mine.

For many years after that, I allowed my performance on this test to define me. You were either born an athlete or you weren't. The other kids—the kids who could do so many sit-ups they had to be forced to stop because they were taking up too much time—were athletes. I was not. I had no understanding then of all the different ways of being an *athlete*, the many shades and tones and hues associated with that word. I did not know then what I know now, that growing stronger is a lifelong journey of discovery, that where you begin has very little to do with where you end up, that it is showing up and doing the same thing day after day after day that eventually produces results. Figuring out who you are is something you get to do again and again in your life, and on that late-night run, I was just getting started.

Rain poured down my thighs. Mud splattered my calves. The waterlogged trail became a makeshift river, and it was impossible to see rocks and roots. I slid, tripped, righted myself, and forged ahead, feeling the trail from memory as much as seeing it from the dim light of my headlamp. I moved slowly, one section at a time, and made it up the first big hill before taking a right on Tarklin Branch. The puddle that was filled with tadpoles and frogs in summer was indistinguishable from the trail. I stomped through it, then shimmied down slick boulders before reaching another stream with rocks that were strategically placed for crossing. Pausing momentarily, I tried to decide how best to balance. Quickly realizing the futility of that effort, I plowed through the creek, then headed up the hill that leveled off for a minute before the final, steep ascent. My feet were icy, my legs numb. And I was running out of steam.

Then, up ahead, through the fog, I caught sight of something moving swiftly away from me. At first glance, it appeared to be a wild animal. But it was too tall. Too agile. And then the beam of my headlamp landed on a giant, soaked, pink bunny. I had felt so utterly, blissfully alone on the trail that

I still could not make sense of what I saw. It had to be a mirage. Clearly, I was dying of hypothermia. Or exhaustion. Or maybe I was drowning. But then it came to me: I was seeing a costumed runner on her final ascent. Perhaps if my mind had initially registered her as a human, the moment would not have seemed so magical, but for just a moment, I had been visited by a miraculous, pastel woodland creature, and that was the vision my brain chose to hold on to.

Follow the giant bunny, I told myself.

I crested the hill just as she turned right and headed toward the parking lot. I knew where I was now. Directly in front of me was a wide field that overflowed with phlox and bluets and daisies in the spring. Tonight, the field was eerie and dark. Still, in my delirium or perhaps my state of heightened perception (and who is to say which is which, really?), I could see them there—the blues and purples and yellows and greens that would, in a few short months, signal the beginning of another season, a season of fresh possibilities. I paused there, took a few deep breaths, and listened to the silence that was broken only by the sound of rain on leaves. And then, oddly refreshed and inspired by the presence of the ethereal rabbit, I sprinted down the gravel road to the parking area, where a hearty group of race officials cheered me across the finish line.

The course had been tough, but rain and cold aside, if you had asked me then if I wanted to run it all over again, I would have said yes. Perhaps it was the adrenaline, the thrill of running through the woods at night, the thrill of knowing that the girl who could not do one sit-up in fourth grade was not too shabby after all. After I passed the finish line, though, I noticed the numbness in my hands and feet, the icicles forming on my gloves, so I headed to the shelter where we were served mugs of hot soup, Halloween candy, and bananas. I downed my snacks and headed to my car, where, blaring the heater, I stripped off my wet socks and shoes and shirts and replaced them with the dry clothes I had brought before heading home. It would take a hot shower and a good night's sleep under a pile of quilts before I truly felt warm again, but the dreams of being led out of the dark, wooded forest by a spectral bunny would stay with me for years.

The next day, I got an email saying I had placed third of the women in my age group, and I had won a beautiful hand-made piece of pottery. I did not know how many women were in my age group, and I did not ask. It is highly possible that there were only three, and that I was last of those three, but I have learned that it is best to celebrate your successes while you can, so I drove directly to the race headquarters to retrieve my prize. I had been running small races on and off for years, but I had never won any prize in any athletic event, unless you counted the Fourth of July pie-eating contest I won when I was eight (and, even then, I was declared the winner by default after the real first-place winner vomited chocolate cream pie onto the table). I knew that the main thing I had going for me as an athlete was that most other women my age had too much sense to be out running in the woods in the dark in the torrential rain when the temperature was dipping dangerously close to freezing. Still, I supposed that counted for something. Gumption mattered. It wasn't better than skill or ability or God-given talent, but it was something, a special power I could nurture and keep on reserve for whenever things got hard.

Truth be told, I excel at only a few things—gum-chewing, for example, or tossing peanut butter biscuits into an aggressive buck's mouth through the barn door slats. I can whip up a decent quiche. I can make a nice bar of homemade soap. I am good at sumo squats and holding plank position. I am good at layering clothes in cold weather and filling long pauses in conversation. However, at almost every other task I have ever attempted, I am not excellent but not terrible either. I am mediocre. This is not a popular thing to say. We live in an age where being mediocre is worse than being terrible, even, because at least if we are terrible at something (like singing, for example) we can believe that we don't even need to attempt it. For everything else, we have come to expect the grown-up version of a participation trophy for everything we attempt: You are excellent! I am excellent! We are all equally excellent all the time at all things! There is so much pressure in this quest for excellence that we may have lost our ability to appreciate the perfectly average, absolutely acceptable, but in no way extraordinary things. We have lost our ability to tell when we have a good idea and when we do not. Here is a case that illustrates my point:

A few years ago, we mated our Nigerian dwarf doe, Loretta, a black-and-white Nigerian dwarf goat, with our Nigerian buck, Merle. After the act was complete, we duti-fully noted Loretta's expected due date: 145 to 153 days after conception. However, when her due date grew near and then passed, we checked our math again. The date was correct, so we were worried. What if her babies were in trouble? What if *she* was in trouble? But when I placed my hand on her stomach, I felt a definite flutter-rumbling. Plus, she seemed perfectly fine. She was eating and drinking and doing all manner of goatly things like grazing and head-butting other goats. Finally, I googled "Nigerian dwarf doe pregnant overdue." The sheer volume of internet discussion surrounding this topic was astounding. I read and read and read until, finally, there in the midst of all the other dialogue about ectopic pregnancies and inductions and C-sections and such, I discovered the truth: *pseudopregnancy*.

Also known as false pregnancy, pseudopregnancy can be caused by successful mating that ends in an early, spontaneous abortion, or it can happen when a doe has never been pregnant, even, occasionally, when she has never been exposed to a buck—a blessed, virginal event. Regardless of the cause, a doe with this condition may accumulate fluid in her uterus, a condition known as hydrometra. She also may actually produce pregnancy hormones and may, therefore, have a positive pregnancy test. She is not faking—not exactly. She is *misbelieving*, committed to the *idea* of pregnancy. This condition may continue for months until, one day, the pseudopregnant doe releases the excess fluid in her abdomen, resulting in a "cloudburst," a sudden gush of liquid from her body. The pseudopregnancy is over, and the doe's body returns to its pre-not-pregnant condition. It is a loss, to be sure, but imagine how much lighter she feels with all that unnecessary fluid gone. Imagine how free.

Why do I mention this? What does Loretta not being pregnant have to do with writing and publishing? Everything. We talk about writing like we are giving birth. We are pregnant with ideas—with the seeds of stories and poems and essays and articles and everything in between. We post "Happy book birthday!" all over social media when our friends publish books. We make our book covers into birthday cakes. We talk about our books being "brought into the world" as if forceps and suction cups were required. We understand how we must first conceive a story and then love that seed of a story before it is anywhere close to a completed story, how we must believe in it long before it is fully realized, before it is loved by anyone else. It is from this deep belly of faith that all great books are born.

However, there are times when we cling too stubbornly to things we need to release, when our faith in the work we have been doing has been misplaced. Here is a hard truth about the writing life: No matter how talented you are, even if you attended the best MFA program in the country and even if you have spoken at every AWP conference and have been published in all the top-tier journals and God herself blurbed your last book, which sold for ten figures and is now a miniseries, somewhere along the way, you are going to write some mediocre stuff. We are all, at one point or another, going to strive to say something beautiful and eloquent and profound, and we are going to fall short. Or, rather, we are going to be *average*.

Sometimes the best stuff you write will languish in your files indefinitely, and your more average work will get picked up more quickly. Chances are, some of your work, bad, good, and in between, will never find an audience. So while it is important to believe in your work, to trudge through multiple drafts, to give everything you write its due, it is also important to separate your writing life from your publishing life, to learn to evaluate your work's potential somewhat objectively and wisely calculate how much time and energy you will devote to certain people and to certain projects.

Of course, we must write all the stories—the good, the bad, the bad ones that will someday be good, the bad ones that will never be good but are our only way through to the better ones. And perhaps we need to write that one thing to find our way to the next, the thing we never saw coming. Perhaps in the writing we will learn to forgive the people who have harmed us. Perhaps we will learn to forgive ourselves for our mistakes. Perhaps we will pay homage to someone or someplace that has shaped who we are and what we believe. Perhaps we will capture memories that we want to hold on to so we can revisit them when we need them. All of these are good and worthy goals in and of themselves.

However, not every story needs our unflagging commitment, our tortured, torturous attention. If we just keep at it, we think, we will eventually get it right. We just need to spend another six or ten or twenty years of our lives tweaking it a bit, and then the story will be good to go. Sometimes, this is true, but occasionally our deep bellies of faith betray us, trick us into believing that the stories we have been coaxing and prodding and encouraging—and, well, frankly, slapping and stomping and waterboarding—have a life in them that they simply do not. I know this false optimism well because I have been there many times myself, and I have seen many other writers get so bogged down with one story that they are immobilized. They can write nothing else. They can think of nothing else. But one of the hardest lessons of the writing life—of life in general, really—is realizing when you need to move on. With each passing year, I realize that my time for doing the things I love is not as long as it used to be, so I strive to get better at cutting my losses before I am frustrated and bitter and discouraged. Perhaps a piece of a discarded story will seep into my next story. Perhaps it will not. But if I cleave too blindly to any singular concept, I may cheat myself out of the joy of discovering those new truths lurking just around the bend.

In *If You Want to Write*, Brenda Ueland encourages writers to explore their passions and write with abandon, without concern for what others will think. "The only way to find your true self is by recklessness and freedom," she says. Further, she references Van Gogh, who once said that one should not disregard the mediocre because, when it comes from a genuine place of imagination and feeling, the mediocre "already means something." In other words, the act of creating is valuable in and of itself. Whether or not it will/should be published is another matter. The word *average* implies that we are all in this together, all on the same level, part of a community of human beings doing the best we can in the moment. Therefore, if we can keep in mind that there is no shame in being average, that, in fact, *most people are average at most things*, then perhaps it will be a bit like trying and trying and trying to get pregnant for so long that you forget you are trying and then one day—voilà!—a baby! How wondrous! A new and unique and totally marvelous creation.

Yes, yes, of course, you say. This makes practical sense because I am not only a writer. I am a complex human being who also wants other things. I want to hike El Camino. I want to tour the forest canals in Wales. I want to go kayaking in Acadia, birding in Costa Rica, biking through the Sonoma Valley. I want to see the Northern Lights and Willie Nelson live in concert one more time. I want to make my own kombucha and Manchego, to take a wine appreciation master class. I do not want to spend valuable time consumed with projects that are not taking me where I want to go. But how do I know the difference between an idea that just needs refining and one that is simply full of water, a pseudopregnancy? When is it time to give up on an idea?

This is an excellent question, one I cannot answer for you. In the spirit of Ross Gay, perhaps I might simply ask you in return: Does this story or idea in and of itself delight you? If so, keep writing it. Keep tending it. Keep loving it. But if you find that it is weighing you down—that, as with a bad boyfriend, you dread every single moment you spend with it, but still you keep hoping without any tangible reason to hope—it is time to consider stepping back. Put your work somewhere safe for a few weeks or months or even years, and turn your full attention to something brand-new. There are so many stories, so many ways to get at the truth. Look for the other ways in. Then, after those weeks or months or years, if you still feel the story calling to you, go back to it. See if you feel the same way.

I have heard you should do this with shopping. If you see an outfit, say, a dress, that you think you love, don't buy it right away. Leave it on the rack and go home, and if you are still thinking about it days later, go back and get it. But what if the dress is the last one in my size or in that particular color? What if someone else buys it? Granted, this is a risk you will take, and, therefore, you must buy into the notion, at least a little, that certain things are meant to be, and certain things are not. This sometimes works for me and sometimes doesn't. For one, the minute I try not to think about something (like a pint of Ben and Jerry's toffee coffee crunch or a ridiculously expensive but very soft dress with lovely front pockets in the perfect shade of blue), it's the only thing I *can* think about. For another, sometimes I am on a dress deadline and need that new outfit *right that minute* because I have a reading that evening and I recently dyed my hair the loveliest shade of lavender and the only other appropriate outfit I have is bright red which now clashes with my hair . . . and, well, you get my point. What works for me may not work for you, and what works some of the time may not work all of the time, but putting a dress or your work aside for a bit is worth considering, especially when the writing process has become dispiriting. The work should be hard, but it should not be joyless, and if it is, it is time to move on.

Over the years, I have set aside three almost-complete manuscripts and countless stories and essays, including one about my bushwhacking friend Susan. Susan and I were taking a writing workshop together when I wrote about how, after class one evening, we went to a West Asheville bar called Jus One More. I was in my early forties, and my children were all in various stages of growing up and leaving home, and I was figuring out who I was going to be once they were all off on their own. The bar was one of the few spots in Asheville that had remained untouched by the bohemian, Paris-of-the-South movement of recent years. The gravel parking lot was lined with pickups with gun racks in the back windows and dog cages in the cabs. Inside the bar, a guy wearing a "Jesus Hates Yankees" T-shirt leaned against the jukebox as Hank Williams Jr. belted "Whisky Bent and Hell Bound." Through thick smoke, I could just make out two pool tables and a chalkboard above the bar where someone had written BANNED followed by a long list of names. The bathroom contained only a toilet and a table with a container of hand-sanitizing wipes.

As you can see, I am still intrigued by the place, and if I were any good at fiction writing, perhaps I could create from this place a short story, but, alas, I am not. As a memoir piece, it was too all-over-the-place, about too many things or maybe not enough things, but, in any case, the narrator had no insights into why she was there. Thirteen years after writing this piece, I can see these flaws, but I don't plan to revise it because I am no longer drawn to that narrator. She is too far gone from me now, so this story now lies in what I think of as my own little literary graveyard, the folder of dead stories I keep like a literary version of Ben and Jerry's

"Flavor Graveyard" (RIP White Russian!). Still, every now and then I think of that night at Jus One More, and I pull up the document and read that story because it reminds me of the good parts of the old, less self-conscious Asheville, the Asheville that has now been replaced not just by new bars and restaurants and music venues but by some new sensibility that doesn't leave much room for the Appalachia of my childhood. It also reminds me of when I first started taking my writing seriously, about how Susan encouraged me, about how I was just beginning, at that late hour in my life, to realize who I was outside of being a wife and mother. And though that story is destined to remain in my literary graveyard, look at it here, seeping into this new story, reconfigured, reimagined.

Say we accept the premise that some of our stories are going to be stunning and some are going to be dead in the water. What, then, do we do with the others—the imperfect, beautiful, flawed ones we still believe in, the ones that keep us up at night, the ones that will not leave us alone? When I am struggling with finding the rhythm in my stories, I sometimes print them out and write questions for myself in the margins: *So what? What is the larger takeaway? What is it you want to say here? What work do you want this passage to do?* Perhaps because I have been commenting on student writing for so many years, this process of printing out my documents and writing in the margins allows me to leave my writer brain for a minute and enter my "teacher" brain, the one that can more easily see what is lacking in a story. Of course, it might work just as well for you to comment on a Word or Google document or even to write within your document using a different colored font, something I occasionally do when I know a section I am working on needs *something*, but I'm not yet sure what that something is. MORE HERE I might write in red font and all caps in the middle of a page. ANOTHER BEAT. WHY DOES ANY OF THIS MATTER?

If you are no longer drawn to a storyline, ask yourself if there is still a nugget in there—a paragraph or two or even a single line that you still feel drawn to. If so, copy and paste it onto a blank page and use it as a writing prompt. Start from there. You may be surprised where this old line takes you. This process is, in a way, like running a trail backward. At first, it is disorienting to go uphill where you usually go downhill, to approach the creek before the cemetery, the hitching post that is normally on your left on your right, the tree that forms a perfect circle on your left and not your right. You are taken out of yourself, out of the pattern you have come to expect and to rely on. Then, gradually, if you open yourself up and let it be, you will find that it is glorious to see the woods in just this way, from this new lens through which everything old looks new.

Becoming comfortable with unexpected outcomes, with twists and turns you could not have imagined when you first began writing, extends beyond the page and into the business of writing as well. Writing requires us to delight in our craft even when that work is hard, even when "success," whatever that is, is elusive, but while writing is often a solitary act, the process of finding an agent or publisher and working with editors and copyeditors and public relations people and marketing people and so on to bring a story or book to publication is very much a collective effort. If you are lucky, you will find people who will work with you to make your work better. They will offer valuable insights and expert advice. They will take your work to the next level. Such has been the case with 95 percent of the people with whom I have worked.

Occasionally, however, you may reach an impasse in which your vision for your work and the vision of the people around you do not mesh, in which case you may find yourself back at the beginning again, trying to figure things out on your own. And so I offer a word of caution here: no matter how anxious you may get to see your work on the printed page, do not leap impulsively into the first opportunity that presents itself. Carefully evaluate your options. For a publisher, ask yourself: Will this press offer me the support I need in terms of editing, marketing, etc.? Does this press nominate books for literary awards/prizes? Does this press publish other books I will be proud for my work to be associated with? Will this press keep my book in print? Et cetera. For an agent, ask: Is this the best person to represent this work? How will she and I work together? What can I expect her to do? What will she expect me to do? Is this person invested in me for the long haul?

Perhaps it is the nature of memoir writing that makes the professional connections we forge seem so personal. When we work with editors and agents, we enter into a covenant where we confess the truth of our lives and invite them to help shape the words on the page and, thus, the way we understand our own lives. When the fit is right, the process is a well-choreographed strength workout. Everything— the squats, the lunges, the deadlifts, the rows—all comes together into one fluid dance, and at the end of the routine, we are sweaty and worn out but happy and stronger for it. When the workout is not well choreographed, however, it is akin to inadvertently signing up for a CrossFit challenge when what we really needed was a good restorative yoga session. We are left depleted and discouraged.

My first agent, the one who quickly and efficiently sold *Flat Broke*, was pleasant and friendly. However, after *Flat Broke*, we repeatedly tried and failed to come up with a new work that we both felt had merit. A year or so later, it was evident that all progress in that regard had stalled. She had stopped offering any meaningful feedback on my manuscripts, and perhaps, to be fair, I wasn't writing anything worth commenting *on*. It became clear that, if we stayed together, I was never going to publish anything else again.

Still, I hung on for two more years and became increasingly frustrated and disillusioned. What was wrong with me? Had my first book been a fluke? Was I really just not cut out for this work? After all, publishing one book means you're on your way, right? It means you don't have to start from scratch each and every time. It means you have someone in your corner helping you shape your ideas and then advocating for your work because they care about your career and your future as much as you do, right? Well, ideally. But sometimes, for whatever reason, things don't turn out that way, in which case you may need to cut your losses and move on. In that event, you can and probably should allow yourself a limited period of time to feel dejected and demoralized. Personally, I think three weeks is a good amount of time. It allows you to grieve without giving you time for the type of full-fledged meltdown that could interfere with your writing life and your actual life. Then, after a suitable period of mourning, get up and dust yourself off and get back to the business of creating.

Go back to the trailhead. Remember all the reasons you began this journey in the first place. Then put one foot in front of the other and start again with that same level of joy and wonder you felt back then, when everything was fresh and you were green and the wilderness beckoned to you. "Why are we reading," Annie Dillard asks in *The Writing Life*, "if not in hope of beauty laid bare, life heightened and its deepest mystery probed?" Why, indeed. And why are we writing if not in the hope of being eviscerated, purged of all we are in the hope that there is something just beyond us that we cannot yet fully see?

The trick is to slog through dark woods and murky memories, through the mud of first drafts and second drafts and third drafts, to release anything and anyone who is holding you back, and finally, if you are lucky, to follow the fantastic pink bunny and emerge on a glorious hillside where everything finally makes sense.

There is your truth, splayed out on a mountaintop for all the world to see.

YOU CAN DO ANYTHING
FOR A MILE

Channeling Your Inner Stallion

Throughout my junior year of high school, I ran with a Walkman the size of a small box of tampons strapped around my neck. The machine pounded against my chest while Quiet Riot's "Come on Feel the Noise" blared in my ears. Back then, I had two running partners. One was my best childhood friend, a high-achieving, do-things-by-the-book sort of person who, I understand, still runs with the same athletic grace and precision today. Another friend, a do-things-any-way-but-by-the-book sort of person, ran with a lit cigarette hanging out of her mouth. Blowing out puffs of white smoke, then gulping in Virginia Slim menthols tinged with oxygen, she sprinted a mile and half from school to downtown. Wheezing, I caught up with her just in time for her to suck down another cigarette before sprinting back to school.

One would think that these first running experiences would have discouraged me, but even though I wasn't a particularly good runner, I loved running. I loved the sweatiness, the exhaustion, the freedom, the way my angsty, anxious thoughts simply passed right through me, like ghosts. *Thought ghosts.* In the years during and after college, I walked more than I ran, but after the births of my three children, when I was in my thirties, I began running again. I did a few 5k and 10k races, and then, in the throes of a pre-midlife crisis, I decided to train for the Bethel Half Marathon, which happened each October in a small community in Haywood County, about an hour's drive over the mountain from our home. Back then, I had no concept of resting in between runs or of the value of "off" days. I thought more was always more, and so I ran sixty miles a week, at all hours of the day and night and in all sorts of weather—floods, high winds, blistering heat, blizzards. I ran when I had a stomach bug and when I had strep and when I had the flu.

In the mornings leading up to the race, I ate four or five bowls of Grape-Nuts and drank a few cups of coffee before taking the kids to school. Then I drove around my running route, noting the mileage and periodically pulling over to plant Gatorade bottles in the bushes along the way. Back at home, I stuffed power gel packs into my shorts pockets and headed out to do a five-mile route, which I would complete two times with a couple of bathroom breaks along the way. Roughly two hours later, I would arrive home, too exhausted to do anything else the rest of the day.

During this time, I made many like-minded running friends. They advised me on all the basics—the most runnable trails, the most cushiony shoes, the thickest socks, the most moisture-wicking shirts, the latest training guidelines.

Gordon, a former high school classmate I had recently
become reacquainted with, gave me a copy of the Runner's
World *Complete Book of Running*. The book became my training bible, and I religiously followed the advice therein.

I learned to "dig deep," just like the book said. I drank
gallons of water and ate pounds of oatmeal and black beans
and pasta. I tried also to visualize that I was a stallion running "tirelessly, with grace, style, and strength." However,
try as I might, I could not see myself as a "wedge" cutting
"effortlessly through the breeze." Which part was the tip?
My feet? My head? Exactly how large was the wedge? The
image just didn't work for me, so I settled instead for visual-
izing limping across the finish line as a crowd of enthusiastic
onlookers cheered me on.

The day of the race, I woke exhausted. I had shin splints
and plantar fasciitis. Now, of course, I realize I had over-
trained, that there is such a thing as overtraining, but then, I
thought that sort of fatigue was necessary. Thus undeterred,
I set out before dawn with David and our two sons in tow.
The parkway was covered in fog as we crossed over and into
Haywood County, and by the time we got to the foot of the
Blue Ridge Parkway, a cold drizzle fell. Conditions were not
ideal, but I had said I was going to do this thing and I was
going to do it.

I had new navy shorts with a trim that matched the bur-
gundy of my top and a pocketful of different-flavored gel
packs—strawberry and watermelon and vanilla. If I looked
the part, I could do it. Or so I believed. By the time I arrived
at the starting line, rain gushed down the street and pud-
dled in the potholes. I probably would have backed out right
then and there had it not been for Gordon, who was there
with his running group to do this race as a "warm-up" for

an upcoming marathon. All confidence and smiles, he had oodles of races under his metaphorical belt. After giving me a pep talk, he moved to the front of the crowd, and I took my place at the back of the line. When the starting gun sounded, there was no turning back.

We ran past farms and up hills and along the Pigeon River, past snarling German shepherds and yapping feists. It was fall, and the oaks and maples were especially resplendent that year, and for the first several miles, I thought, *I've got this. I'm doing it.* And then, somewhere around mile ten, I crashed. My legs were no longer connected to my body. Every movement required extreme concentration. The rain, which had abated earlier, returned. A gray mist covered everything. People flew past me until, eventually, I saw no one, not even the water people or support crews. I ran alone on a deserted country road, and I just hoped I was heading in the right direction.

Then, just when I was about to give up and walk the rest of the way, in the distance, Gordon appeared jogging lightly yet briskly away from the finish line, in my direction.

"How are you doing?" he asked when he reached me.

"Not so good," I said.

As he fell into step beside me, I thought I would cry. Then I thought I would vomit. Miraculously, I did not actually do either. Finally, at mile twelve, at the *One Mile to Go* sign, he asked, "This is it. Do you want to sprint?"

Are you fucking kidding me? I wanted to ask. But I refrained.

"Listen," he said. "It's just a mile. You can do anything for a mile."

In the coming moments and weeks and years, I would hear him say it again and again. This notion that I could break a challenge down into segments was a skill I learned right then and there, and it would carry me through many tough days in the future, times when I could not see where I had come from or where I would end up, only what was right in front of me. *You can do anything for a mile.*

Propelled by how earnest Gordon was, how optimistic and upbeat and hopeful, I dug deep. I put one numb foot in front of the other until finally I could see—through the mist—the gym, the banners by the road where we had started all those hours ago, and, at last, on the pavement, the smudged chalk arrows pointing to the finish line. I could also see that the school parking lot was empty except for the finishing judges, and I spotted my David and my sons, three fuzzy specks huddled together by the white line across the ground. When I finally dragged to the finish, I had been running for almost three hours. Later, I would discover that all the post-race snacks had been put away. The awards ceremony was over, and the other runners had all gone home.

"You ran this in two hours, so and so minutes," the judge told me as he recorded my time. "That means you should run a marathon in . . ."

Trying to do the math, he looked at his watch.

"Oh, no," I said. "That means I should *never* run a marathon."

I had signed up for this race, and I had given it my best shot, but even I could see that my future was not in competitive running. Thinking back on that day now, though, I don't remember so much how hard it was. I remember most a simple act of kindness from a guy who could have run the whole race twice while I was tying my shoes and pinning on my race bib. *You can do anything for a mile,* he had said. And it was true. What he did not add but what I know now to be true is this: You can do anything for a mile *so long as you want to badly enough.*

You have to *want* to run 13.1 miles for no other reason than to know you can do it. You have to be willing to push through burning thighs and stomach cramps and a searing pain in your left calf. Even though you may believe with all your being that you are a feral hog, you have to mentally transform yourself into a stallion. You have to visualize the finish line and hold on to that image even when it seems that all the other runners have finished ahead of you. Running is hard. You have to know that this is true for everyone, even the seasoned runners, even the ones who make it look easy. If it were easy, it wouldn't be worth doing.

And so it is with writing. The ones who make it across the finish line are the ones who find their own pace and stick with the race even when it seems they are losing. I recently read that musician and poet Patti Smith believes she has created her best work after age fifty-seven, which rocked my world. Smith, who challenged our complacency with "People Have the Power" and mesmerized us with *Just Kids*, felt her best work came *after* these remarkable works. In a society that most loudly celebrates early and big and dramatic successes, this notion that the longer we do what we do, the better we get at it, seems somehow radical, but I have begun to consider how absolutely vital all of my training—including my failures—have been. What if everything I have experienced up until this moment has simply been a warm-up? What if I am only on mile five of a half-marathon that I will complete on my own time and in my own way?

When I was a teenager, I had a harmless but aesthetically problematic accessory nipple removed from my right breast, and while I was prone on the exam table, my bare nipple numb and exposed, the doctor asked me what I wanted to do with my life. Up until that moment, I had never really considered that question. I was sixteen years old, and I thought my whole life was happening right then and there. It had never once occurred to me that I might need to prepare for more than what was right in front of me. However, the doctor was waiting for an answer, so I said the first thing that came to my mind. I was failing both geometry and chemistry but passing English, and I had just been appointed editor of my high school newspaper.

"I might be a writer," I said.

The doctor was my father's friend. He was tall, mostly bald, and so thin his white lab coat swallowed his torso. Wrapping his stethoscope around and around his arm, he stepped back from the table, peeled off his surgical gloves.

"But in order to write, you need to have something meaningful to say, right? I mean, you have to do something interesting with your life, have interesting experiences."

In retrospect, I'm not sure whether he was engaging in philosophical discussion or simply pointing out the obvious, that, at this point in my life, I did not, in fact, have anything interesting to say. In any case, this was not a conversation I wanted to have while in this awkward position, but since he had brought it up, I told him I thought you couldn't just be interesting, that you had to be able to write in unique and interesting ways. Still, he had a point, and for the next thirty years, every time I looked at the tiny scar on my breast, I asked myself the same questions: Had my life been interesting enough? And how did I write in ways that other people might find interesting?

For many years after high school, I did not write anything other than essays required for school. My undergraduate degree was in sociology, and I did not begin creative writing in earnest until the last semester of my first graduate program, when I wrote a creative thesis, a collection of poorly developed, overly sentimental vignettes about growing up in Appalachia. I was thirty-three years old with three young children, and though by then I did have a few interesting things to say, I was not yet able to say them in a unique way. In other words, I had not yet found my voice. That process would take even more time. It would take years of studying craft, and writing and writing and writing until, eventually, I became more confident, more aware that when I sat down to write, a voice approximating my own would appear on the page.

Then, when I was forty-eight years old, I began an MFA program at Vermont College of Fine Arts with a group of other students, mainly women, who were either twentysomething or exactly forty-eight. I cannot explain why this was, but it was. Perhaps twentysomething and forty-eight are the ages when we have the most to say, or perhaps it is when we give the fewest fucks about what people think about what we say, but in any case, there I was with a bunch of women my age, and many of us had grown kids, and some of us were in recovery from addictions of various kinds, and others of us drank like crazed college students because it had been so long since we had been out of our houses without our partners and kids, and a couple of us were completely normal, well-adjusted humans, but the rest of us knew that those in the latter group really weren't going much of anywhere with their writing because, well, they didn't have much to say. Which made me think, once again, of the good doctor of my youth and of the race I ran on a foggy mountain morning at a time in my life when I drank more Gatorade than water. Had my life been interesting enough?

I graduated from my MFA program the summer I turned fifty, and my book came out the following January, and though at the time it felt like a rapid transition from publishing in tiny, obscure journals, I realized that, really, the process had begun back in that doctor's office, back when I was still blaring Quiet Riot while jogging the streets of my hometown. My path to success, it turned out—or success as I had defined it for years, in terms of a book—had been painstakingly slow.

"You're a late bloomer," my husband told me after my book came out.

And he was right. It had, indeed, taken me years to figure out exactly how to say what I wanted to say. In writing a memoir about losing my home, I had simply found the situation that would allow me to tell the deeper story I had been trying to tell since my first stabs at it almost twenty years before—the story of a deep connection to home and family, a story firmly rooted in Appalachia. That story, I believe, was richer and more layered than it would have been if I had told it when I was twenty-five or even thirty-five, but it remained essentially the same story I had always been trying to tell.

The writing journey is long, and it is easy to burn out. On those days when you have gotten five rejections in your inbox and are struggling to come up with even one meaningful, articulate sentence, and you feel like you might start sobbing to a perfect stranger (or, worse yet, on social media), it is time to remember how you feel when you are out running. Unless you are one of those people who fell out of the womb and started running, you are going to have days when your knees ache and your Achilles tendon hurts and your plantar fasciitis is acting up or even days when, for whatever reason, you just cannot find your rhythm. You just aren't that into it that day. In fact, you can't for the love of God remember why you ever thought running was fun in the first place.

On days like that, you have to remember the days when the weather is top-notch and your knee is bionic and the leaves on the trees are radiant and you are a freaking gazelle. On those days, running is the best thing you have ever done, the only thing you have ever wanted to do. Runs like that don't happen every day, which is why they are special, why you have to take big gulps of air, breathe them in deeply and hold them there, close to your heart and to your gut. Those runs are food. They fortify your spirit. The other runs, the hard ones, are just practice runs, training your body and mind to go harder and faster and longer, preparing you to appreciate the glorious simplicity of an easy run.

The same is true with writing. I have heard other writers say they have written remarkable works in remarkably short periods of time—an evening, an afternoon. This sort of talk is both fascinating and ridiculously discouraging. I have been writing for years. Why does it still take me so long? Why does it never get easier? After my book came out, people asked me how long it took to write, and I told them it took me roughly a year, from the beginning of my MFA program to the following summer. What I did not think to say then but what I realize now is that I had been writing that book for most of my life. That's how long it takes anyone to write a book—a lifetime.

Almost a decade ago, I wrote a brief lyrical essay titled "Looking Glass." I sent it off to some places, and it ended up being published in an anthology of southern Appalachian literature and in this really beautiful book of poems and photos in commemoration of the anniversary of the parkway called *Blue Ridge Parkway Poetic Visions*. I was thrilled that I was done with this topic. I was going to go on and write something grittier, edgier, something more worthy of what I thought good literature was at the time. But, clearly, I was not done with the subject of mountains and hiking and such. Home. Yearning for home. Longing for a past that is almost gone but not quite. I can see the one story of my life unfolding even there, even here.

If, as Ann Patchett says, writers spend their whole lives retelling the same story, the challenge then lies in staying the course and making the same old narrative feel new each time. These are monumental tasks, tasks that require patience and fortitude and rapt attention to the world around us, to subtle changes in the landscape—the auburn tinges of a maple leaf, the yapping feist on the hill, the gentle lull of the Pigeon River as it ambles west toward Tennessee—and to the voices inside our own heads that have the power to transform us into strong and graceful stallions, into wedges slicing swiftly through the wind. For me, the challenge on the trail has never been to be the first or the fastest. The challenge has come in sticking with it, in persevering long enough to see myself get better and braver.

Every time we take a stab at writing, we are honing our skills, winding our way around and around and getting closer and closer to our truth, and all the things I have ever written—the stories I have published in tiny literary journals that no one has ever heard of and the snippets of things that never got published anywhere—have found their way back into my work at some time or another, in some form or another. Which is all to say that when you commit to anything hard—running or writing or cake-baking or playing chess or learning to play the cello—you have to prepare for the long haul. You have to be good to yourself, to take care so that you don't burn out before you see what you are really capable of doing.

One of my favorite Peloton instructors, Adrian Williams, is fond of saying, "Squeeze your glutes, or no one else will," which, if you think about it, is the perfect metaphor for taking care of yourself in general. You must attend what needs attending, mind your own peace of mind, preserve your own joyfulness because no one else is going to do it for you. In between all the writing and thinking about writing and feeling guilty about not writing and contemplating all the things you should have or could have written, you must take breaks and immerse yourself in the dailiness of living. After all, the writing life requires that you actually have a life outside of writing, so nourish your writing but also yourself and the ones you love. Do whatever simple thing feeds your spirit. Pick a bouquet of flowers for your writing desk. Play some Bee Gees. Go to a concert. Drink a glass of wine. Take a long walk. Get a deep-tissue massage. Make a pot of hearty potato soup.

On those days when you feel like you need some extra inspiration, consider immersing yourself in a different art form. Watch a film. Go to a play or a museum. Cook a special meal. (Sometimes, when I cannot think of anything to write about, I flip through my recipe box and write about a particular food—the associations I have with it, the memories it evokes. I have written stories inspired by seven-layer salad, chocolate chip cookies, cream cheese braids. Each one of those brings up a certain memory and a certain feeling associated with that memory.) I have writer friends who also paint with watercolors or throw pottery or crochet or write songs or play the dulcimer, but I can't do any of those things. Instead, I wander into an art gallery. I switch up my Spotify playlist and go on an extra-long run in the woods. I go to an outdoor concert. I make a batch of soap in my slow cooker. Sometimes I visit my favorite local pottery shop. Outside the store, a rack of slightly imperfect pottery sits next to a wide, gurgly creek, and I park in the shade by the creek and peruse the mugs and vases and plates and butter dishes until I finally settle on a piece—a green mug with a mountain bike imprinted on the side, a soap dish, a toothbrush holder.

This very tactile experience inspires me in a way I can't quite articulate. I suspect my fascination with this shop has something to do with the fact that the creek, an offshoot of the French Broad River, is the same creek that ran by my cabin door when I attended a summer camp just down the road. Ten years old, shy and awkward, I was constantly homesick, especially at night when the final strains of "Taps" sounded over the hillside. As I lay in my bed, conjuring my mother's canary-red lipstick, the singsong lilt of her voice, the scent of her Jovan musk, the creek kept me company, lulled me to sleep. This creek is both literally the same creek and the same creek of my memory—cheerful, soothing. Perhaps my love for this shop also has something to do with reconnecting with beautiful things, with stoking my sense of awe and wonder. As I pick up a bowl and run my hands over the smooth surface or grip different mugs to try out the handles (do I want a thumb rest or no?), I think, *a human being made this*. How astounding is that? How astounding are we?

"Good for you," I tell myself every time I finish a hard ride or a long run. "Way to go!"

For the longest time, I did this without even realizing it until one day my daughter heard me.

"Are you talking to yourself?" she asked.

"Why, yes, I am," I said.

And then I realized that I give myself pep talks all the time—when I finish grading a particularly daunting set of research papers, when I finish cleaning up the kitchen after a big family meal, after I hit "send" on a story submission. In late middle age, I have finally learned to celebrate my successes. *Good for me.* And good for you as well.

We are all still here doing this hard, beautiful thing we love.

THE BEAUTY OF THE QUESTION

Embracing the Wilderness Within

Our cabin is surrounded by more than forty acres of dense woods. Just below a waterfall and above the goat pasture, however, is a grassy area with a small firepit. There, for fourteen months during the pandemic, I hosted socially distanced s'mores parties like it was my full-time job. Our daughter, Alex, had been living at home for more than a year, and our two sons and their partners were in and out, and we gathered outdoors with friends we hadn't seen in months and family we had only seen from a distance. We could have lived in our yard if we had wanted, and this unscheduled, quiet time was a rare and precious gift—all of us there, all of us safe and well.

Next to the fire, I set out a card table covered with a blue tablecloth and held in place by a bouquet of daffodils or azaleas or lilies or whatever was in bloom alongside a massive jar of hand sanitizer. I stocked coolers with beer and fizzy drinks, passed out insulated tumblers filled with wine. I organized three varieties of graham crackers and a slew of gourmet chocolates on a slate cheese tray. With a thick piece of chalk, I labeled the chocolates—milk chocolate, dark chocolate, white chocolate filled with caramel, cookie crumbs, almonds, orange bits, strawberry jam, toffee. It was extravagant, ridiculous even, but in a world where we had few options, a chalkboard filled with possibilities was a small comfort.

Sitting six feet apart, we leaned into the fire, rotating our sticks as we debated the finer points of roasting the perfect marshmallow. Our two sixteen-year-old dogs, Hester and Pretzel, weaved in and out of our legs. We tossed them graham crackers and bits of marshmallows, and when they stumbled too close to the fire, we gently shooed them away. When we got tired of making s'mores, sometime around September, we ordered an outdoor pizza oven. We bought a giant blue party tent to shade us from the sun and keep us dry in the event of rain. We bought long outdoor tables and filled them with pizza toppings—pesto and marinara and white sauces, caramelized onions, marinated artichokes, sun-dried tomatoes, a variety of cheeses: mozzarella, feta, goat cheese, parmesan, gouda. When we got cold, we bundled in blankets, jackets, scarves, wool caps. When our guests had to pee, we handed them a flashlight and sent them to the bushes around the side of the cabin.

"Watch for snakes!" we called after them as they traipsed into the darkness.

Though we were constantly aware of the grief and devastation around us, in our little world, we were largely untouched by it, and there were moments when these evenings seemed perfectly natural, what normal people might *choose* to do during normal times—like camp, only better because there was no wake-up bell, and we didn't have to sing. Late in the evening, stars filled the sky, lightning bugs lit up the holler, and coyotes and screech owls pierced the silence. It was both magical and perfectly ordinary, and we were learning that ordinary was, indeed, something to be grateful for.

It was too early then to imagine what might come next, when a vaccine might be developed, when we might go back to our classrooms and office jobs, whether we would ever again fly or go to a gym or concert. We drank and talked until we were out of wine or words or both. Then we poked the fire embers and listened to the gurgling of the waterfall. When it got too late or too cold, we fed the dogs the graham crackers, soggy with evening dew, and folded up the tables and chairs. What else were we to do then except hunker down in our separate households and watch the news and listen to podcasts and like social media posts and figure out what to do the next day but never the day after that because the sense of helplessness was overshadowed only by the sense of timelessness? We lived in a liminal space between this world and the next, between what we could see and what we simply needed to believe was there. Time was amorphous, suspended, irrelevant even. We lived beyond time. Who even knew what day it was anymore? What week? What month or year?

Perhaps the one thing that kept us from floating away entirely was the fact that we maintained some routines. Alex's job often required her to meet with interpreters and clients simultaneously, so while she participated in three-way calls, I taught first-year writing and creative writing via Zoom in the adjacent space. By the end of the day we were exhausted, spent, and if it hadn't been for our one-year-old hound Homer, the newest addition to our pack and the only one of our dogs who liked to run with us, we might never have left the house. Every day at 5:00, his insistent pounding on the back glass door (*How does he know it's 5:00?* we asked. *Who gave him a watch?*) alerted us that the workday was over, and it was, indeed, time to go to the woods.

Most days, we chose the trail that ran along the Davidson River near our house, but once or twice a week we headed to DuPont. At Guion Farm, we saddled Homer up with either his Carhartt coat or his running harness (depending on the weather), his leader, his leash, and a hot-pink bag of treats we velcroed to one of the aforementioned items. We then donned our masks and took turns peeing in the portable toilet in the adjacent field, then dousing ourselves with hand sanitizer before switching out our masks for Buffs and heading down Buck Forest Road.

Alex ran in front with Homer, and with her long brown hair tucked under her cap, her black running tights identical to my own, she looked so much like I had when I was younger that time and place buckled and twisted, shapeshifting tricksters, and I no longer knew for certain when or where or who I was. I was six years old running down a wooded path or I was sixteen running along the beach at Kiawah Island or I was thirty-six running along the North Rim of the Grand Canyon, the canyon filled with wildfire smoke, the sky flushed orange. I was both not me and all of me, a woman-girl suspended in time. Pretty soon, Alex and Homer were two specks in the distance. And then we turned onto Thomas Cemetery Trail, and they were gone altogether. Though I was technically alone, if I had needed help, Alex eventually would have noticed my absence and returned for me, and in a world that felt increasingly scary, the woods were, as always, the place I felt most safe. They were, in fact, some days, the *only* place I felt safe.

One day, however, Alex was out of town, so instead of running our usual route, I decided to take Homer hiking in another part of DuPont. We waited until late evening because I figured that, by that time, most of the tourists would have loaded up their mountain bikes and paddleboards and kayaks and headed into town to the breweries. I figured there would be a few people about but not so many as to make me feel like I was hiking at Disney World, as I sometimes did at peak tourist season. However, when I pulled into the Buck Forest access area, the parking lot was deserted. I briefly hesitated. Then I figured I wasn't exactly alone since I had Homer, so I put him on his leash, and we set out walking on Conservation Road. We crossed the top of Triple Falls, wound around the Lake Julia Spillway, and headed up the hill. From there, we hung a left and took a back route to the airstrip.

At any moment, I expected to see another person—someone who had come in from one of the other parking areas, perhaps—but even when we saw no one, I kept going. Then, in a curve at the bottom of the airstrip hill, Homer threw up his tail, pressed his nose to the ground, and zigzagged back and forth across the road. *A scent.*

"I sure hope that's a deer you smell," I said.

Then, just as we rounded the bend, I heard something scurry up the bank to the right. Homer turned and pointed, tail up, ears up, nose straight ahead. I followed his gaze, and there, in the woods just off the trail, stood the largest black bear I had ever encountered in the wild. She moved a few feet and stood behind a pine tree, her eyes locked on us. I knew that black bear attacks are extremely rare, and when they do happen, most often, mother bears are reacting to real or perceived threats to their cubs. I hadn't seen any cubs. Still, most of the bears I had encountered on the trail quickly scooted out of sight. This bear had run initially but was now standing her ground. She stared me down or, perhaps, stared Homer down, but in any case, her gaze was chilling. My limbs twitched with adrenaline, with the urge to flee.

"Do not run. Do not run," I whispered to myself over and over.

Homer, on the other hand, clearly had no intention of running. He remained perfectly quiet and still, his eyes locked on the bear. He was a hound dog, and he had done his job of pointing out the bear. It was up to me, I supposed, to figure out what to do next. Growing up in a family of deer and bear hunters, I had heard the black bear encounter guidelines a million times. *Make noise. Keep your eyes on the bear. Walk calmly away. Move to higher ground. Do not make a high-pitched sound.* I clapped my hands a few times, but the bear stood firm. Perhaps it was too little, too late. Maybe that was what you were supposed to do *before* you saw a bear and before *it saw you.* I couldn't remember for sure, but I continued clapping as I walked, one foot in front of the other, without ever taking my eyes off the bear. Homer walked next to me, his entire body tense and ready to spring into action if needed. The bear, however, remained exactly as Homer had left her. Her eyes followed us up the mountain until we rounded the last bend, and she disappeared, or we disappeared, depending on your perspective.

Somewhere near the top, I pulled my cell phone from my pocket and called David. He could hear my heavy breathing before I said a word.

"What's wrong?" he asked.

"A bear is stalking us," I said.

I described how massive the bear was, how she was just staring at me, how there was no one else around. Bears aren't supposed to just *stare*, I said.

"Where are you?" he asked.

We had reached the top of the mountain. To our right was the cabin where one of the rangers lived, and in front of us was the old airstrip. Normally, people gathered at the end of the airstrip to see the view, but there was no one in sight and no car at the ranger's house. There was also, thankfully, no sign of the bear, and as my heart rate began to slow a bit, it occurred to me that the term *stalking* might have been a bit rash.

"No. I think we're okay," I said just as I lost cell service.

I sighed and tucked my phone in my pocket.

"We're on our own now, buddy," I said to Homer.

He glanced nervously behind us, then up at me.

"You're okay," I told him. "We're okay."

Apparently, however, I was not convincing. In the coming weeks, whenever we approached this area, he would stiffen, stop, look pleadingly at me: *Remember? Remember what happened the last time we were here?* Now, as we made our way down the mountain, he walked with his warm flank pressed against my right leg. To reassure us both, I complimented him on what a brave boy he had been, what fine bear-spotting skills he had, and so on, and soon he grew more confident. By the time we reached the covered bridge near Triple Falls, he was jogging, and I was running behind him, struggling to keep up. When we reached the parking lot, I expected to find it deserted and was surprised to find that there were a few people milling about. We had not been completely alone in the forest after all.

Later, in the safety of my car, it occurred to me that something extraordinary had just happened. I was awestruck by how close I had come to the bear, how long I had been able to observe her. I considered how regal she had been, her thick, black fur, her taut body and knowing eyes, the silent stillness of the woods, the way the mountain laurel hung over the road, the soft, pink petals scattering beneath our feet. I wondered what she had been thinking, whether she was afraid, whether there were babies close by that I had not seen. I wished I had taken time to drink in that moment. I wished I had taken a photo.

I wished . . .

I wished . . .

I wished . . .

Remembering that magical bear encounter of my childhood, I wished most that I had another chance to be brave, joyful, delighted by her unexpected presence. I wished I could see her for the first time all over again. Later, I even tried to go back and find her. I walked the same route at the same time of day, but she was not, of course, where I had left her. Here on the page, however, I get to see her once again. I get to be braver, more joyful. I get to linger in the space where anything could have happened and simply drink in the beauty of that moment.

This fluid sense of time is both a gift and a challenge for memoir writers. How do we exist both within a certain time (the "real time" of the story) and beyond it? How do we define the temporal limits of our stories? Fiction writers, it seems to me, have an easier time with determining where they are in a story. If they get into a bind, the protagonist can get murdered or married or arrested or discover a treasure or a cure for a rare disease—any number of exciting things.

But in memoirs, where the truest beginning is perhaps the writer's birth and the truest ending is perhaps her death, the story is ongoing until, well, it isn't. Endings, therefore, are especially troublesome. The writer is still living her life, still discovering the meaning of all that has transpired. How does she know when to end? And, even more importantly, how does she know *how* to end?

When I was writing *Flat Broke*, I originally ended the book in Puerto Rico for no real reason other than that I was in Puerto Rico for my MFA residency when I finished writing it. I had fallen in love with the spectacular waterfalls and beaches and forests, not to mention the songs of the coqui and the rich, creamy avena we ate for breakfast each morning and the strong coquito we drank one evening as we watched the sunset from the rooftop of a house in San Juan. My trip to Puerto Rico was simply the last wonderful thing that had happened in my life. There was, of course, no good reason to end a book about Appalachia in Puerto Rico, but that's what I did initially. Then my wonderful and wise Sourcebooks editor, Anna Michels, suggested that I end where it all began—back in the North Carolina hollow where we lived. And so I went back to the drawing board (i.e., my computer).

For days, I struggled to come up with a more fitting conclusion. Something was always happening at our farm. Baby goats were being born. Chickens were dying. Blueberries were ripening. The creek was flooding. Once, my husband shot a copperhead in our kitchen. Another time, coyotes surrounded our evening campfire. How did I know which moment to choose? How did I end something that seemed to be unfolding every time I sat down to type? I'm still not sure I chose the perfect ending, but I had been writing long enough by then that I knew what questions to ask, and I returned to the advice Connie May Fowler gave me during my first semester at VCFA: *Find the heartbeat of your story.* In other words, find the driving force. Ask yourself where the power of the story lies.

Where was the heartbeat of my story? As soon as I asked the right question, I knew the right answer: My grandmother had died just as the events I chronicle in the book began unfolding, but she had had an enormous influence on my life, and I was continually guided by her wisdom. Her presence was powerful to me as I was writing the book and, I hoped, on the pages themselves. It was evident to me then that I should end there, with my grandmother and the very last time she visited me.

To clarify, when I say I knew the "right" answer and the "right" question, I mean for me, for this particular story. I mean that I have come to understand how instructive the questions themselves can be, how crucial my comfort with *discomfort* is to my development both as a human and as a writer. However, I do not mean to imply that there is ever one right way to end—or, for that matter, write—a memoir. During writing workshops, sometimes my students will debate how a story should end, and then they will turn to me and wait. It usually takes me a second or two before I realize that they think that I know the answer—the *right* answer—and they are waiting for me to give it to them. I am always sorry to disappoint.

"I love that you are wrestling with this," I say.

Inevitably, they roll their eyes. It is not an easy thing to hear. We want to know the right answers, but even more importantly, we want to believe there *are* right answers, that someone else has them and can give them to us, but asking someone how to end your story is like asking someone which is the correct way to hike a loop trail. It depends. It depends on whether you would rather see the mountain laurel thicket first or last, whether you would rather the river be on your right or left. It depends on what you think of as the beginning and what you consider to be the end. It depends on the *so what*, what really matters to you. In writing, there are no right answers, only different ways of approaching the questions. How you end has everything to do with who you are and what you believe, and how could I possibly tell you that? And so I return again and again to the questions, to the beauty of the unknown.

Once, when I was doing a reading for *Flat Broke*, someone in the audience, a former Peace Corps volunteer, raised his hand and offered one of those comment-questions that, at first, leaves you worried about where it is going. I can't remember where he had served, but in any case, he described a remote village somewhere, let's say in Cambodia, where his life had been, by necessity, pared down to the essentials. The adjustment had required a monumental shift in his thinking, but over time, he had come to appreciate the slower pace of day-to-day life, the things he learned about himself, the meaningful connections he forged with the people around him.

Later, as his service came to an end, he began to worry that, back in civilian life, he would forget the lessons he had learned here. He knew he would embrace some comforts from his old life—flush toilets, for example, clean drinking water straight from the tap, hot showers—but he wanted to maintain an appreciation for a quieter life, a life without all the stuff and the go-go-go mentality of his previous life in the States. In my book, I had written about having a similar epiphany, about how my life had changed after we had lost our home, how I had learned to live a simpler, fuller life than I had before. Though we had lived vastly different lives, this man and I had that in common.

"What is it about your life now that you want to keep when everything changes?" he asked me.

At the time, I was in the midst of my pared-down existence. Sure, I had sold a book, but the income from that was hardly life-changing, and the notion that it would be possible for my life to be different one day was not one I had even entertained. I don't remember my response. I'm sure whatever I said was not particularly insightful because I am not given to on-the-spot profundities. In addition, my own personal reckoning and all the resulting discoveries were still unfolding. But now I think the truest answer was—and is—I do not know.

If, as memoir writers, we accept that our truths are still evolving, that we have not yet discovered all there is to be discovered, how does this impact our writing? And, in particular, how does it impact the ways we end our stories? When I was completing the critical thesis for my MFA program, my mentor was Robert Vivian, a wildly talented poet and essayist and wonderfully generous human being who encouraged me to experiment with form. Bob and I communicated mainly by email, but as the semester was coming to an end, we scheduled a phone conference. It was November, and I didn't have reliable cell service at my house, so I sat in the car in a grocery store parking lot with the car motor running and the heat cranked up while we talked.

Bob listened intently while I described my struggles with my thesis, an exploration of memoirs in vignettes composed entirely in that same experimental form. It was tricky to pull off and even trickier finding the proper ending. I wanted to write a wise and learned conclusion that encapsulated all I had learned about what made the vignette form so uniquely moving. However, none of the many attempts I had made had felt quite right. Before I had talked with Bob, I had not realized how scared I was that I would never find the right conclusion, that I would, therefore, never graduate, that I was already a has-been writer before I ever really got started because I sucked at endings. I was tearfully prattling on in this way when Bob said something that changed everything.

"What if you don't write a conclusion?" he asked. "What if, instead, you just open the whole thing up?"

In other words, what would happen if I simply posed possibilities? Thus freed from the task of knowing all the answers, I simply asked on the page all my remaining questions about how the vignette form might extend beyond creative writing to other forms of writing, especially academic rhetoric. My conclusion, then, was a series of questions—dozens of them!—all beginning with "what if." Bob's insistence that ambiguity had its place was at once both a beautifully simple and radically complex idea, one that would revolutionize both my work and the way I looked at the world. In basking in the unknown, I was finally able to find my way to what felt like a fitting conclusion. Hopefully my ending led the reader to new possibilities, but, more importantly, it led *me* to new possibilities, which is to say that it did the thing that writing should do: It changed me. It changed how I thought about writing. It changed how I *taught* writing. It changed how I saw the world.

Now, whenever I approach what feels like the end of a story, I ask myself the questions Bob taught me to ask: What if we were to reimagine each ending as a beginning? What if we didn't have to know all the answers? What if we allowed room for readers to breathe, to settle inside our stories and discover themselves there? What if we considered possibilities instead of certitudes? What if we understood that everything we write reflects only what we believe *in that moment* to be true? What if we learned to be comfortable in the space between wondering and knowing? What if we acknowledged the fact that we are all, at every level of learning, still floundering, still grasping at truth? What might it feel like to continue reaching upward, gaining strength, gathering momentum? In what ways would our notions of truth shift and change? In what ways would we be empowered? In what ways would we be freed?

Lately, my running song of choice has been "Beautiful" by the Americana quartet the Two Tracks. In the song, the speaker asserts that the story of an afterlife is simply that—a tale we have created to assuage our fears of dying. Aside from that one line, the song is filled with rhetorical questions that celebrate the beauty of the here and now. Over and over, the song asks if the afterlife can be more beautiful than this one. The line "Can it be any more beautiful than . . . ?" is completed with various examples of earthly delights—the Pacific Ocean, redwood forests, the Blue Ridge Mountains, New Orleans, Mississippi, good whiskey, you and me. Taken together, these questions propel us toward an imperative: Do not miss the beauty of this world. What begins as a series of questions about the nature of beauty thus becomes a charge to live our lives more fully here and now.

Powerful questions change us. They reshape the ways we think and the ways we move in this world, and as writers, we must learn to ask those hard questions that lead us to deeper understandings. Each and every time we sit down to write, we must embrace our doubts, probe our vulnerabilities. We must wait expectantly for the next good thing to come. We must (metaphorically speaking, of course) stare down wild bears. We must return to Brenda Ueland's imperative: To give freely of ourselves, to write with compassion and generosity. And in those moments when we doubt ourselves, when we feel like imposters, a bunch of no-nothing wannabes, we must remind ourselves that there is tremendous freedom in the partly known, the unknown, the can-never-be-known.

We need not have all the answers. We need only to seek passionately and earnestly the beauty of this world. Even now, as I worry that I do not know enough about writing or about the outdoors or about life in general to be writing this book, I remind myself that these words are as much for me as they are for you, so that I may come to know this imperfect, magnificent world more fully. Even with all the things I do not yet know, I belong here. *You* belong here. We belong in this space where joy and courage and curiosity and empathy and fortitude collide and spark a force greater than any element of craft or trick of the trade. So, we wait for the right questions to arrive, for the right ending to reveal itself so that we can move together from this moment to the next one. The acorns have begun to fall. What am I going to do with that? What are you? What wild, wondrous adventure comes next?

I once heard Billy Collins lament the overuse of the use of the word *suddenly* in poetry. *Suddenly*, so the thinking goes, is a cop-out word, one you use when you can't think of a better one. It is too easy and rarely accurate because things that seem sudden are hardly ever sudden at all. More often, we simply cannot yet see the next thing coming. It is that moment when, after all those weeks and months and years of writing something, the truth beneath the story finally reveals itself. You see, at last, what the story needs to be, what it was meant to be all along. Perhaps it isn't exactly sudden, but it *feels* that way, and so, I would argue, it is true.

For me, the pandemic—at least the throes of the pandemic—ended this way. One minute we were hunkered down roasting marshmallows and raising baby chicks and stockpiling yeast and bread flour and dried beans and rice, and the next minute, just like that, vaccines were as plentiful as the recently surfaced cicadas. In the spring of 2021 the whole world opened up—or so it seemed—and we believed then that the period of upheaval and uncertainty was over for good. Of course, we were wrong. We didn't anticipate the variants to come or the fact that so many Americans would choose not to get vaccinated. We did not yet know that the first phase of the pandemic would end like so many other stories, with more questions than answers. Still, in that moment, the moment when we believed we were untouchable, on a hillside in the Montford area of downtown Asheville, Alex and I sat on a hillside listening to roots musician Charley Crockett. Charley's sound was timeless, ageless. He was bluesy and country and folksy, a lot of soul with some rock-n-roll. He was hard to define, hard to pin down, his deep drawl as much New Orleans as Texas, as much Hank Williams and George Jones as B. B. King, as much 1940 as 2021. We had thought this would be a small affair—a few folks venturing cautiously out after months of isolation. We had thought we were dipping our toes in the water. But we were wrong. When we arrived, the venue parking lot was already full. We followed the crowds and eventually found a parking place on a nearby tree-lined residential street. As we were walking to the gate, a young woman rode past and called to us out her car window, "Hey, are y'all going to see Charley Crockett?"

"Yes," we yelled back.

"Whoo-hoo!" she hollered and peeled away.

Hell, yeah. We were going to see Charley Crockett. Not only that, after fourteen months of semi-isolation, we were going to be closer than six feet to other human beings who were not in our immediate household. It was both a little scary and a lot thrilling. The amphitheater was outdoors—a small, elevated stage surrounded by a dance floor. Beyond that was terrace seating and, beyond that, a grassy hillside designated for lawn seating. I had expected a subdued affair, masked ticketers and families clustered six feet apart. The word *gradual* came to mind. The words *partial opening.* After all, just weeks before, someone on Twitter had called Asheville the "maskiest city in the U.S." It was supposed to be an insult, but Ashevillians responded with pride. We were, indeed, as passionate about mask wearing as we were about craft beer and Chacos and vegan menu options.

However, just days before the concert, Governor Roy Cooper had announced an end to mask requirements for indoor and outdoor gatherings, and the concert organizers had opened the previously limited show to full capacity. When we arrived, the beer lines had already spread across the hillside, and the crowd was already amped. No one wore a mask. And there were other signs that life was returning to normal or, at least, Asheville normal: food trucks and portable toilets. Young people tripping. Gray-haired stoners swaying blissfully to the beat. Patchouli-scented babies. It took us a few minutes, maybe a few more than a few, until we felt it too, the powerful undercurrent carrying us all away from whatever dark, dismal place we had been. We spread our blanket on one of the last available spots on the grass, threw off our shoes, then plopped down to take it all in.

Chairs were not allowed, but people had chairs. Smoking weed was not allowed, but people smoked weed. Standing in front of people was frowned upon, but people did it anyway. We had all been inside so long we didn't know how to act. Trump was no longer president, and we might never Zoom again. Like Charley, we refused to be contained. We were ageless, timeless, genre-less or, perhaps, we were all genres. To paraphrase Bob Dylan, we contained multitudes.

On the dance floor, a middle-aged, yellow-shirted guy danced next to the stage, his style a sort of hallelujah shimmy with passionate arm raising and pointing to the heavens. Alex and I were mesmerized by all the variations of this move—the slow-mo churchy sway, the high-stepping do-si-do, the dizzying tilt-a-whirl, the jumping bean (aka the Avett Brothers dance). Below us was the girl who had called to us earlier from her car. Barefoot, she wore bell bottoms, a white midriff blouse, a silver-studded belt. She was from 1972 and 2021 and every year in between.

In the coming weeks, before the delta and omicron Covid variants began widely circulating, my kids would all settle back into their own lives, and I would settle into mine. I would go to restaurants and stores. I would book flights and hotel rooms. I would once again bleach my hair, book optional medical procedures. I would grab beers with my friends and prepare for teaching actual live human beings instead of dark boxes on a Zoom screen. My life would return to being as normal as it ever had been. I could see it all coming. The past fourteen months had been full of sorrow and worry and fear. They had also been full of family and dogs and bears and outdoor dinners and long treks in the woods, and I had been changed in ways I could not yet fully know. What was it I wanted to keep? What if I could take just one thing with me?

What if . . .

What if . . .

What if . . .

Of course, it was too soon to know all the answers. My story was still unfolding, yet one truth was clear: We were entering a new season of possibilities, and though I could not yet see where I was headed, I knew that you never walked out of the woods the same person you were when you walked in, that once you had stared down wild bears and raced after pink bunnies and zipped with Tinker Bell, you were forever changed. And how beautiful was that? How beautiful were we?

Soon the sun set, the stage lights turned neon pink, and Charley crooned a deep bass balm for our spirits that were so very tired from doing nothing. He sang of love, of home, of forgotten people, of trouble with the law, and the yellow-shirted guy danced, and the teenagers tripped, and the old people swayed, and all around us, Asheville hummed. The whole world hummed.

The world was no longer on fire.

We were on fire.

QUESTIONS FOR FURTHER EXPLORATION

1. Discuss your relationship with fear. When do your fears serve you well, and when do they get in your way? What is your greatest fear? Where does it come from? What strategies do you have for keeping it at bay? What does it feel like in your body? When/where/how does it overwhelm you? Now, imagine for a moment that you weren't afraid. How might your life be different? How might *you* be different?

2. Discuss the nature of truth as you see it. Are there different degrees of honesty, and, if so, what are the gray areas? What makes a story true or untrue? Can a memoir contain both lies and deeper truths? In what ways?

3. What is the most daring thing you have ever done as an adult? Why did you do it? What did you learn about yourself? In what ways have you carried that knowledge with you since?

4. Discuss your relationship with physical strength/stamina. When in your life have you felt strongest? When have you felt most vulnerable? Why and how were you shaped by these experiences?

5. Discuss the role of imagination in your life. What did you dream (literally or metaphorically) when you were

a young child? What is the most imaginative thing you have done in your waking life as an adult? What other things do you dream about doing? What, if anything, is holding you back?

6. Describe a moment in your life when you were lost (again, literally or metaphorically). Where were you? Who was with you? How did you come to be lost? How did you come to be found? And what did you learn along the way?

7. Make a list of questions you have about any topic. These can be ridiculous or serious. They can focus on one area, or they can be wide-ranging. The only requirement is that you cannot currently know the answers. Try to get ten or twenty questions. When you are finished, trade questions with someone you know. Now, take their list of questions and see what new questions arise for you from those. In other words, what questions do you have about their questions? You can do this on and on, in an endless game of round-robin with questions.

8. Do you agree with Brian Doyle's assertion that, no matter how hard we try to communicate effectively, we invariably fail in our attempts to express the depth and breadth of our emotions and experiences? Why or why not? How might acknowledging the inherent shortcomings of language change both our relationships with others and what we bring to the page?

9. Drawing inspiration from Ross Gay, vow to spend every day for the next week noticing things that delight you. Each day, make a note of one, simple thing—a box turtle in your flower bed, a blackberry patch you came upon while hiking, a new song you discovered, a phone call with an old friend, a batch of freezer jam you made

that turned out especially well. Freewrite about this for no more than one page. The point here is to capture the mood and the tone, the essence of the delight. Keep it simple. Do not attempt to make a cohesive story. Do not use a thesaurus or run a grammar check. Do not go back and edit old entries. This is not a stepping stone to anything else. Think of each entry, each delight, as whole and complete, as worthy in and of itself. The goal here is not a polished final product. The value is in the practice, the practice of noticing, of cultivating and expressing gratitude for all those quietly astounding moments that fill your life with meaning. At the end of the week, share your responses with at least one other person. Notice how your delights multiply when you share them.

BIBLIOGRAPHY

Butler, Robert Olen. *From Where You Dream: The Process of Writing Fiction*. Grove, 2005.

Dillard, Annie. "Total Eclipse." In *Teaching a Stone to Talk*. Harper-Perennial, 1982.

Doyle, Brian. "The Way We Do Not Say What We Mean When We Say What We Say." *The Sun*, March 2016, www.thesun magazine.org/issues/483/doyle-say-what-we-mean.

Garden, John. *The Art of Fiction: Notes on Craft for Young Writers*. Vintage, 1991.

Gay, Ross. *The Book of Delights*. Algonquin, 2019.

"Memory and Forgetting." *Radiolab*, June 7, 2007, www.wnyc studios.org/podcasts/radiolab/episodes/91569-memory-and-forgetting.

O'Brien, Tim. *The Things They Carried*. Mariner, 1990.

Patchett, Ann. *The Story of a Happy Marriage*. Harper, 2014.

Rich, Louise Dickinson. *We Took to the Woods*. HarperCollins, 1970.

Ueland, Brenda. *If You Want to Write: A Book about Art, Independence, and Spirit*. Sublime, 2014.

ACKNOWLEDGMENTS

Thanks to the friends mentioned here—Karen, whose courage and gentle wisdom continually inspire me to be a better version of myself; Susan, whose bravery in the face of unmarked trails, rattling rattlesnakes, and classrooms full of rowdy ninth-graders astounds me; Meg, who did not, in fact, let me die on a mountain biking trail (though she did let me tumble a few times); O.J., who models decorum and quiet determination and discourages my tendency to freak out in high places (or anywhere else, for that matter); Ann, who is not the slightest bit scared of bears (I know, I know—I owe you one!); and Margaret, who has been my decades-long adventuring companion on the trail and in real life. Thanks also to the friends who do not appear in these pages but who have patiently listened to me over the years as I have droned on and on about my four favorite topics—running, hiking, biking, and dogs. I hope the occasional beer I bought you was some compensation.

Thanks also to my friend and colleague Lori Horvitz, who is always up for exchanging work and who asks the best questions. You are the nicest, shrewdest critic.

A huge debt of gratitude to all those teachers, both those I have named here and those I have not, who nurtured my love of words early on and who believed I had something valuable to say even when there was no actual evidence to support that sort of optimism. I carry your faith with me every time I walk into a classroom.

Thanks also to the Vermont College of Fine Arts and to my mentors and fellow students there. The two years I spent with you all changed the direction of my life, and even though I do not do snow or ice or winter well, I would once again fly through a blinding snowstorm just to hear your beautiful words in person again.

I am also hugely indebted to Tommy Hays and all the wonderful students and faculty in the Great Smokies Writing Program at UNC Asheville. The impacts of this community on my writing and on my life are immeasurable.

I am also grateful to those literary journals and editors who have supported my work over the years and especially to those who have published portions of these essays in earlier versions, including *Brevity, Still, Literary Mama, SalonZine, SlowTrains,* and *New Southerner.*

Tremendous thanks also to everyone at Trinity University Press who had a part in bringing this book into being, especially my editor, Steffanie Mortis Stevens, whose enthusiasm, encouragement, and careful attention to my work restored my faith in my own writing practice at a time when I needed it most. Steffanie, your insights have been invaluable, and I am forever grateful.

A huge thanks also to my copyeditor, Daniel Simon, who taught me, among other things, that *treeing walker* and *seven-layer salad* are not capitalized! Thank you, Daniel, for your wisdom, your humor, and your patience.

Finally, to my husband and children: Thank you for letting me drag you into the woods and onto the page with me. Your love and support are everything.

A graduate of the Vermont College of Fine Arts, Jennifer McGaha has led writing workshops for writers of all ages and experience levels in a variety of settings for more than two decades. Her memoir, *Flat Broke with Two Goats*, was chosen as a 2018 Big Library Read for OverDrive. Her work has appeared in many magazines and literary journals, including the *Huffington Post, New Pioneer, Lumina, PANK, Chronicle of Higher Education, Brevity, Bitter Southerner*, and others. A native of Appalachia, she lives in the North Carolina mountains.